FROM "BACKWARDNESS" TO "AT-RISK"

SUNY Series, Youth Social Services,
Schooling, and Public Policy

Barry M. Franklin and José R. Rosario, editors

FROM "BACKWARDNESS" TO "AT-RISK"

CHILDHOOD LEARNING DIFFICULTIES AND THE CONTRADICTIONS OF SCHOOL REFORM

Barry M. Franklin

State University of New York Press

The cover photo entitled "An Old Fashioned Boys' School," is reproduced from the collections of the Library of Congress.

Published by
State University of New York Press, Albany

For information, address State University of New York
Press, State University Plaza, Albany, N.Y., 12246

Production by Diane Ganeles
Marketing by Fran Keneston

Library of Congress Cataloging in Publication Data

Franklin, Barry M.
    From backwardness to at-risk : childhood learning difficulties and
the contradictions of school reform / Barry M. Franklin.
        p.   cm. — (SUNY series, youth social services, schooling, and
public policy)
    Includes bibliographical references (p.) and index.
    ISBN 0-7914-1907-X. — ISBN 0-7914-1908-8 (pbk.)
    1. Learning disabled children—Education—United States—History.
2. Mentally handicapped children—Education—Georgia—Atlanta—Case
studies.   3. Learning disabled children—Education—Minnesota—
Minneapolis—Case studies.   I. Title.   II. Series.
LC4705.F73 1994
371.91—dc20   93-26760
                                                                   CIP

10 9 8 7 6 5 4 3 2 1

In memory of my mother and father

Ruth Franklin (1912–1964)
Philip Franklin (1902–1972)

Contents

Foreword

"To See a World in a Grain of Sand/And a Heaven in a Wild Flower/Hold Infinity in the Palm of Your Hand/And Eternity in an Hour." So wrote the religious poet and English romantic, William Blake, in the early nineteenth century in a poem entitled "Auguries of Innocence." Like romantics in every age, Blake contrasted the innocence of youth with the evils of corrupt social institutions. He assailed churches that lacked compassion, schools that governed through fear, and a social order that produced poverty in a land of riches. As he wrote in his famous *Songs of Innocence and of Experience*, "How can the bird that is born for joy/Sit in a cage and sing/How can a child when fears annoy/But droop his tender wing/And forget his youthful spring."

Barry M. Franklin's history of low-achieving, troubled, innocent children is sometimes chilling, recalling Blake's horror at society's indifference to human suffering and the baleful influences of modern institutions. For all their ostensible attempts to help children, America's public schools have frequently clipped the wings of youth, including deserving fledglings just emerging from the nest. Our schools have often tried to honor their historic commitment to include everyone, despite the corrosive power of racism or social class injustice. How they have responded to those who consistently fail, however, is an unhappy tale, whose many dimensions form the core of this insightful book.

With a poet's eye but historian's sensibility, Franklin deftly recovers missing pages of the past. He provides the reader with valuable historical perspective on current policy debates on "at-risk" children. Ours is not the first generation to worry about, care about, and remain perplexed about students who perform poorly, behave inappropriately, or learn differently. Throughout this century citizens have held ambivalent attitudes toward these children. Many citizens of good will still want to help them, knowing they deserve neither pity nor wrath, but kindness and effective schooling. At the same time, citizens have often worried more about how "backward," "special," "exceptional," "learning disabled," and now "at-risk" youth can disrupt the rhythms of the regular classroom. Segregating those who are different has been common.

Beyond setting the story of special education in its widest social and intellectual contexts, Franklin demonstrates how to see a world in a grain of sand. The reader occasionally meets some individual students, whose plight in gaining a satisfactory education reveals the high hopes and sober realities of twentieth-century schools. Franklin rightly judges schools by how they treat their most maligned students, a high moral standard worthy of emulation. Victoria Poor, Eleanor Gross, John Bell, William Kirk, Otto Friedrich, and Bob Hartzwell are not household names. Yet their experiences at school take us beyond the world of educational research and theory to the real world of practice.

Across this century, educators and administrators generally relegated to segregated classes those children who were hard to teach and difficult to manage. This enhanced the administrative capacity of the schools while placing these children at the margins. Franklin does not see the world in simplistic terms, with an evil empire of teachers oppressing the poor and outcast. Teaching particular children can be daunting, if not overwhelming. Educational researchers, social scientists, administrators, lay reformers, parents, attorneys, professional associations, and community leaders on school boards have often been major actors in shaping school policies. The failure of the schools to do better reflects poorly not just upon teachers and schools but upon these people and the larger society.

Franklin's sympathies lie with those pupils most poorly

served by our nation's schools. This population is far more diverse than the "backward" label popular at the turn of the century or the "at-risk" label currently fashionable. Moreover, his close examination of the fate of special programs in Atlanta and in Minneapolis during this century demonstrates how understanding schools on the grassroots illuminates the larger landscape. Without losing sight of national trends, readers get an intimate view of how policies were shaped and implemented in these two systems.

If history is any guide, contemporary efforts to eliminate segregated special education classes will encounter considerable resistance. As Franklin notes, the labeling of children, while under some assault, is ingrained in educational thought and practice, reflected most dramatically in ability grouping and tracking. Even middle-class liberals (whose children often attend the best public schools in a community) cannot be counted on to favor current movements for "inclusion." Everyone knows the value of a designer label.

The common school ideal of the nineteenth century emphasized the idea of inclusiveness, at least in theory, for all white children. Few educators or social activists today believe all children can or should master a common body of knowledge. This, too, makes unlikely the possibilities of building a modern common school with high expectations for all. Emphasizing individual or group differences rather than our common humanity seems more popular than ever.

From "Backwardness" to "At-Risk," however, concludes on a note of cautious optimism, hopeful that we may be entering a more enlightened age. While fully aware that the needs of professionals and institutions often take precedence over the needs of children, Franklin ends with a welcome song of hopefulness and anticipation. He raises the same questions posed by William Blake, who wondered whether schools could serve their students well: "How shall the summer arise in joy/Or the summer fruits appear/Or how shall we gather what griefs destroy/Or bless the mellowing year/When the blasts of winter appear."

William J. Reese
Bloomington, Indiana

Preface

No problem has proved more persistent or intractable to those who have managed our schools during this century than has the question of what to do with children who are difficult to teach and often at the same time troublesome to manage. Such students, no doubt, have always been present in our schools. Yet, the working out of two trends, one intellectual and the other social, in the hundred fifty or so years proceeding the turn of the twentieth century would assure that the presence of such children would preoccupy the attention of modern educational reformers, some working in the schools and others working in numerous philanthropic organizations outside the schools.

During the years from the mid-eighteenth through the end of the nineteenth century, the way in which Western intellectuals, including Americans, understood deviance would undergo a fundamental transformation. What was thought at the beginning of this period to represent explicit and willful recalcitrance on the part of individuals requiring coercive punishment, came to be viewed as implicit and unintentional behavior requiring therapy of one sort or another. What was once characterized as criminal, came to be seen as illness. This shift, which we can describe as the medicalization of deviance, would have an impact on a wide array of problems related to social control. One such problem was the management of children. Here, it would lead to the appearance on the scene of numerous child-saving institutions, including the schools. Because of this transformation in our thinking about deviance, schools would begin by the turn of the twentieth century to accept responsibility for children with learning difficulties and other types of low-achievement. Known by a wide range of labels—including backward, mentally retarded, learning disabled, and at-risk, to name but a few—these children would become and remain a central concern of American educators.

During most of the period when this intellectual shift was occurring, America was undergoing an economic transformation to a market economy that would change the complexion of its schools. Two features of this shift—the growth of wage labor and the development of large-scale manufacturing—would act to increase the number and diversity of children attending schools. As a consequence, it was a change that would bring into the schools the very low-achieving children which a medicalized understanding of deviance had prepared the schools to accept. And it was a change that would lead school managers to develop new administrative capacities to provide for these children.

In attempting to deal with growing numbers of children, including children with learning difficulties, early twentieth-century school managers were immediately faced with the task of reconciling their changed circumstances to an existing educational system that was ostensibly committed to the ideal of common schooling. First articulated among mid-nineteenth-century promoters of public education, this ideal characterized schools as institutions in which all the children of the Republic—rich and poor, Catholic and Protestant, immigrant and native-born—would be instructed together in the principles of basic literacy, civic virtue, and democratic citizenship. Restricted as this early system of public schooling was to white children and even sometimes to males, it was from the start an unrealized ideal. Nonetheless, this belief in common schooling soon became and continues to be a moral compass for guiding our educational endeavors. It would consequently lead school reformers throughout this century to attempt to show how the innovations they were promoting at the moment would ultimately advance a more inclusive system of public schooling.

How twentieth-century school reformers would reconcile this ideal of common schooling with an increasingly diverse enrollment is the subject that I will explore in this book. In the chapters that follow, I will examine how school reformers and others throughout this century have sought to adjust their belief in common schooling to the problem of childhood learning difficulties, and what that effort tells us about the now emerging movement for the education of at-risk children.

Acknowledgments

The arguments advanced in this book have benefited from
the wise counsel and thoughtful criticism of numerous individuals. I particularly value the reactions, comments, and suggestions of three colleagues and friends—Herbert Kliebard,
Thomas Popkewitz, and José Rosario. Over the years, they
have both read and reacted to various drafts of the book's
chapters, and have challenged me in various ways to refine my
thinking about the history of American school reform. A number of other individuals have read and reacted to various versions of the book's chapters. They include Beatrice Cain, To-
mas Englund, Ivor Goodson, Elisabeth Hansot, Eleanor Hilty,
Paul Mattingly, Susan Merrifield, William Reese, Theresa
Richardson, Amy Schutt, and Gary Wehlage. I appreciate their
thoughtful comments, criticisms, and suggestions. In this vein,
I am particularly indebted to John Rury whose critical reading
of the entire first draft of this manuscript was exceptionally
helpful in refining and sharpening my argument. Ultimately,
of course, I assume total responsibility for this volume and the
interpretation advanced within.

I am grateful to the following archives for granting me
access to the manuscript collections used in the book and to
their staffs for assisting me in my research: Atlanta Public
School Archives; Atlanta Historical Society; Detroit Public
School Archives; Groves Learning Center; Minneapolis Public

School Archives; Minnesota State Archives, Minnesota Historical Society; New York City Board of Education Archives, Milbank Memorial Library, Teachers College, Columbia University; Social Welfare History Archives, University of Minnesota-Twin Cities; and Southern Labor Archives, Special Collections, Georgia State University.

I wish to thank the Faculty Development Committee of Kennesaw State College for several faculty development grants, which helped support my research and writing. I also wish to acknowledge grants and support from the University of Oslo (Norway), the University of Uppsala (Sweden), the University of Western Ontario (Canada), the Soros Foundation (Hungary), the Institute for Science Education at the University of Kiel (Germany), and the University of Lisbon (Portugal), which allowed me to present earlier versions of the chapters in this book as lectures and seminar papers. I found the comments and reactions to those lectures and papers extremely helpful in writing the final draft of the book.

Throughout the period during which I conducted my research and wrote this book, I was awarded generous release time from my teaching responsibilities. I am indebted to several administrators at Kennesaw State College for those reassignments. They are John Beineke, Dean of the School of Education; Robert Driscoll, former Dean of the School of Education; George Stickel, Chair of the Department of Secondary and Middle School Education; and William Impey, former Acting Chair of the Department of Secondary and Middle School Education.

Throughout my work on this book, I have benefited from the help of Priscilla Ross of the State University of New York Press. I am appreciative of her help in the shepherding of this volume from its inception to its completion.

As always, I have been sustained, energized, and inspired by my wife Lynn, and my children Jeremy and Nathan. Lynn read and offered criticisms and suggestions for each of the chapters. My youngest son, Jeremy, was unendingly tolerant of my frequent need to lock myself away in my study. My oldest son, Nathan, was attending high school when most of this book was being written. His own experiences with that institution were a constant and often poignant reminder to me of why I was writing this volume.

Portions of this volume represent revisions of essays that have appeared elsewhere. Chapter two is an expanded version of an earlier essay, "Progressivism and Curriculum Differentiation: Special Classes in the Atlanta Public Schools, 1898–1923," which appeared in *History of Education Quarterly* 29 (Winter 1989): 571–93. The section of chapter one on the backward child movement appeared earlier in a somewhat different form as a portion of an essay entitled "The First Crusade for Learning Disabilities: The Movement for the Education of Backward Children," in Thomas Popkewitz's edited volume, *The Formation of the School Subjects: The Struggle for Creating an American Institution* (London: Falmer, 1987), 190–209. And the section of chapter three on the work of Strauss and Werner on brain-injured children was drawn from an earlier essay, "From Brain Injury to Learning Disability: Alfred Strauss, Heinz Werner, and the Historical Development of the Learning Disabilities Field," which appeared in my edited volume, *Learning Disability: Dissenting Essays* (London: Falmer, 1987), 29–46. I appreciate the permission of the publishers and editors to include this material.

1

Learning Difficulties and the American Public School:
A Conceptual Framework

During early February of 1974, the *Minneapolis Tribune* published a short reminiscence by Otto Friedrich concerning an incident that occurred some thirty-five years earlier when he was a sixth grader at Green Street School in Brattleboro, Vermont. His teacher, Mrs. Forbes, was a stern and demanding woman who routinely implored her students to exert all their effort and who thought nothing of admonishing or flunking those children who did not live up to her expectations. No one that year, Friedrich reported, felt her wrath more strongly than did a new student, George Grass. George, as Friedrich put it, was "a little slow" or "not quite right." He was a child who today, according to Friedrich, would be placed in a special class. There were, however, no such classes in Vermont in 1940, and so, he was sent to Mrs. Forbes's class. Mrs. Forbes assigned George to a seat in the rear of the room, a place she reserved for her less able students.

During his second week in class, Mrs. Forbes gave a history test, which George did not pass. George in fact, as Friedrich recalled, wrote the same answer, "vegetables," for each question. The next day, after returning the tests to everybody except George, Mrs. Forbes proceeded to read his test to the entire class:

"Listen to this," Mrs. Forbes said, holding up George Grass's
paper and beginning to read aloud from it. "When did the
Pilgrims land at Plymouth Rock?" "Vegetables . . . ." "Who
was Miles Standish?" "Vegetables." "Who was Pocahontas?"
"Vegetables . . . ." "What happened to the witches of Salem?"
"Vegetables."

The entire class, according to Friedrich, began to laugh.
George, himself, began to laugh. Mrs. Forbes then stated that
George would have to do better on the next test. There was,
however, Friedrich concluded, no next test for George. He
never returned to Green Street School again.[1]

A week later, Mrs. Marvin Anderson of Cannon Falls, a
small town just outside Minneapolis, wrote to the *Tribune*
editor to suggest that Mrs. Forbes had not realized that George
had a learning disability. "There are," she said, "many Georges
in the world." Anderson then went on to describe numerous
mistakes that Mrs. Forbes had made in dealing with George.
Children with learning disabilities do better when asked questions in private than in front of the entire class. They do better,
Anderson noted, if they can respond orally instead of in writing. Finally, Anderson stated that George would have per-
formed better if he sat in the front of the classroom where he
could more easily attend to the teacher. Anderson ended her
letter by asking, "What are we as parents and our schools doing
for George?"[2]

During the almost four decades that separate the Vermont
of Otto Friedrich's youth from Mrs. Anderson's Minneapolis,
our view of children such as George Grass has undergone a
major transformation. A child who in 1940 was thought of as
being intellectually slow and was virtually driven from school
by the teacher's ridicule would by the end of the 1960s be seen
as learning disabled and deserving of not only compassion and
understanding but special education. The purpose of this volume is to recount the events surrounding this change, to explain why have they occurred, and to consider how they have
affected the nation's public schools.

The story that I will tell in this book is of more than

antiquarian interest. During the last several years, educators have begun to talk about the need to alter the public school's curricular and instructional programs to accommodate a host of children who they describe as being at-risk of school failure. Although these efforts seem to be just getting underway, the kinds of reforms that are being promoted for these children are quite similar to the special class that Friedrich mentioned and the instructional modifications to which Anderson referred.[3]

The events that transformed students such as George Grass from being "a little slow" to learning disabled can be seen as the first attempt by school reformers to accommodate at-risk children.[4] Since we have already traversed the terrain of school failure earlier in this century, it may be prudent—before we embark again on this endeavor—to consider the initial efforts of America's public schools to accommodate children with learning difficulties.

The place of history in exploring educational policy-making is at best uncertain. We should no doubt like to believe that if we study earlier instances of school reform, we can identify our past mistakes and avoid making them again. Yet, as Emile Durkheim warned us at the beginning of this century, a knowledge of past lapses may not enable us to avoid making similar mistakes in the future. "Since the realm of error," as he put it, "knows no bounds, error itself can appear in an infinite variety of forms."[5]

Nonetheless, exploring the history of this brand of school reform may prove valuable. One of the detriments of studying familiar and commonplace events and issues, Durkheim reminds us, is that we tend to assume a certain inevitability about how things will turn out. Contemporary studies of at-risk children often assume that existing programs of remedial and special education represent the best ways of teaching children with learning difficulties. Examining past efforts at educating children who were difficult to teach will lead us to confront a known problem in a less familiar setting. In this unknown territory we may find that outcomes that we have taken for granted as being inescapable can be otherwise. In other words, a study of past efforts at reforming the schools to accommodate students with learning difficulties can lead us to see the problem of at-risk children in new and interesting ways.[6]

II.

Not unlike other educational labels, the precise meaning of the term *at-risk* is difficult to pin down. Some educators argue that the at-risk label represents the latest in a line of terms that have been used to refer to children with school learning and behavior problems. They equate at-risk, then, with such other labels as *low-* or *underachievement, mild retardation,* and *learning disabilities.*[7] Robert Slavin and his associates, for example, define at-risk students as those "who are presently eligible for special or compensatory education."[8]

Others see the at-risk label as constituting a departure from previous conceptions of school failure. At-risk children, they argue, can include those with high ability and those from middle- and upper middle-class families, children who were usually excluded in earlier conceptualizations of school failure. And the source of the risk, they go on to say, is just as likely to be a faulty and failed school as it is to be a deficit within the child. As Wendy Hopfenberg and her associates note, at-risk students are "those who lack the family, home, and community resources to succeed in schools *as schools are currently constituted.*"[9]

The position that I hold in this book is closer to the first of these viewpoints. There are certainly differences between such categories as low-achievement, learning disabilities, and at-risk. Whereas low-achievement, for example, is a very broad label associated with learning problems of diverse origins, learning disabilities is typically used to refer to learning problems attributed to a central nervous system dysfunction. Similarly, the at-risk category includes children whose school failure is attributed to alienation, a problem that would not normally be considered a learning disability. Yet all of these labels are social constructs that educators and others have coined at various times to address a similar problem—namely, the presence in schools of children who for a host of reasons are difficult to teach and often troublesome to manage. There is, I believe, something to be learned about current efforts to reform the schools to accommodate at-risk students from earlier attempts this century to provide for students with other labels but nonetheless in danger of failure.[10]

The children who we are labeling as being at-risk have been, it seems, a perennial concern of American educators. In his annual report to the Board of Trustees of Illinois' Lake View High School in June 1881, Principal A.F. Nightingale bemoaned the fact that almost sixty percent of the students who had entered the school since its opening in 1874 had failed to graduate. These students did not, he thought, possess "any inherent intellectual incapacity." Rather, they were "pushed, hurried, goaded, crammed in their preparation at the very time when their progress should be slow, steady, and sure." These students, according to Nightingale, had been able to meet the standards required for admission to Lake View. Once they were admitted, however, they were unable to "cope with the studies of the high school."[11]

Nightingale was not alone among the educators of his day in voicing a concern about the academic and social problems that school children routinely confronted. Beginning around 1880 and continuing through the first three decades of the twentieth century, school reformers throughout the country sought, usually with the support of women's voluntary organizations or other private philanthropies, to establish an array of social services to assist children who were experiencing school-related difficulties. Among these programs were medical inspection and other health services, vocational guidance, visiting teacher services, sex and health education, vacation schools, and special schools and classes for the handicapped.[12]

Of all these early social service programs, public school special schools and classes were the forerunners of today's programs for at-risk children. Precisely when these schools and classes first appeared and for whom they were designed has been a matter of some controversy. Writing in 1900, Rhoda Esten credited the Providence, Rhode Island Public Schools with having established the first special class for so-called backward children in 1896. A 1916 survey of education in Cleveland, Ohio, noted that the city had established a special school for delinquent boys in 1876. And Robert Kunzig reported in his 1931 U.S. Office of Education study that New York City had established a parental school for delinquent youth in 1857 and Boston had introduced a program for deaf children in 1869.[13] Notwithstanding this difference in opinion concerning when special classes and schools were first established, the clear champions of this reform impulse were early twentieth-century Progressives.

Some of these first special schools and classes were designed for children who had such clearly defined disabilities as blindness, deafness, and orthopedic handicaps. Other programs made provision for children whose disabilities were less obvious and less clearly defined, including mental retardation, backwardness, and incorrigibility.[14] Despite these differences in clientele, Progressive era school administrators had two goals in mind in promoting this reform. In his 1896 report to the Detroit Board of Education, Milton Whitney, Principal of the Truant School, saw the major contribution of his school as financial: "We are saving the city and state thousands of dollars that would have to be spent to prosecute the boys, criminals in after years, and support them in some of the state penal institutions at a cost far exceeding the amount spent in maintaining this school." Yet, the Truant School was also supposed to help children: "Besides the matter of expense, is it nothing that we save many of these boys from becoming criminals in after years?"[15]

Reporting to the New York City Board of Education in 1920, Superintendent William L. Ettinger noted a similar conflict in the purposes of special classes. When placed in regular classrooms, according to Ettinger, handicapped children not only failed academically but their pride and morale were undermined. In addition, their need to repeat courses and grades that they had failed brought extra expenses to the city. For Ettinger, "the proper classification and segregation of such children was therefore desirable, not only from a humanitarian, but also from an economic standpoint."[16]

Four years earlier, Atlanta's Superintendent of Schools,

Leonidas Landrum, expressed the conflicting purposes of special classes in somewhat different terms. Such classes would, he noted, help the regular classroom by allowing the teacher to do "more effective work with the normal children." But they would also help handicapped children who would be provided "special individual attention along lines suited to their mental growth and development."[17] Difficult to teach children, then, created a dilemma for turn-of-the-century school administrators. As Milwaukee's Superintendent of Schools, C.G. Pearse, saw it, these special schools and classes would "save these children from themselves." Yet these programs, again in Pearse's words, would "save the state from the harm" that these children may bring to the schools.[18]

Public school special schools and classes, then, were created out of contradictory purposes. School reformers promoted these programs to minimize the financial costs associated with educating difficult to teach children as well as the educational burdens their presence in regular classrooms brought to teachers and students alike. At the same time, however, they supported these classes to supposedly help the handicapped. The different and conflicting messages that turn-of-the-century school administrators sent in defending these first special schools and classes have remained as a continuing characteristic of special education as well as other programs to accommodate children with learning problems. No feature of the attempt of educators to accommodate children who are difficult to teach has been more salient in shaping and directing these programs than has been its incongruous goals. As we explore that effort in the chapters that follow, I will pay particular attention to what these contradictory purposes tell us about this enterprise.

III.

If we are to account for the development of public school programs for children with learning difficulties, including today's at-risk students, we need at the outset to explore two distinct but, as we shall see, related issues. First, we need to examine how turn-of-the-century school reformers came to believe that children who were difficult to teach and troublesome to manage were the responsibility of the public schools. Second, we need to explain why these educators advocated the creation of special schools and classes as the vehicle for accommodating these children.

It was not inevitable that early twentieth-century American schools would serve children with learning difficulties. It took a transformation in our thinking and discourse about deviance for this to happen. Our sense of what constitutes a deviant act would have to change from a moral lapse or simple recalcitrance to a socialization failure. And our understanding of how one responds to deviance would have to change from something akin to punishment—namely, inflicting pain or death—to a process of reintegrating the individual into society. In Western Europe, legal reformers seeking to render the system of criminal justice more efficient and enlightenment thinkers who wished to humanize and democratize political relationships began to initiate these changes in the latter years of the eighteenth century.[19] In the United States, similar changes began later and were in midstream in the years surrounding the turn of the twentieth century.[20]

We can see the beginnings of this shift in the thinking of American intellectuals by examining the efforts of the founders of American sociology in the years around the turn of the twentieth century to devise a theory of social control. Such a theory, they believed, was needed to address what they saw as the increasing disorder accompanying the nation's transformation to an urban, industrial society. One of the first to try his hand at this task was Edward A. Ross. Writing in the last decade of the nineteenth century, Ross blamed the discord he saw about him on two factors, which he associated with urbanization and industrialization. First, a growing emigration from Eastern and Southern Europe, he argued, was creating a population that was increasingly diverse in ethnicity as well as in beliefs, values, and attitudes, the building blocks of social unity. Second, the demise of the rural small town meant the end of the one institution whose intimate, face-to-face relationships and like-mindedness in beliefs, had been, he maintained, the traditional guarantor of order in American society. To combat these two destabilizing events, Ross sought, as he explained in his autobiography, "the linch-pins which hold society together." Toward the end of 1894, after about four months of research, Ross went on to say, "I set down as they occurred to me thirty-three distinct means by which society controls its members. This is the gem of my social control."[21]

Modern urban society, Ross argued, lacked such inherent tendencies among individuals as sociability and sympathy, which had in an earlier day provided almost automatically for a sense of social order. To compensate for these natural mechanisms of order, twentieth-century America had, according to Ross, to develop an array of artificial restraints. Among these controls, some, including law and public opinion, operated directly and overtly through the application of sanctions, often coercive. There were, however, other kinds of controls, including education, ceremony, illusion, and ethics, to name but a few, that operated indirectly and covertly through suggestions, feelings, or judgment. Ross believed that these latter, indirect controls were the most appropriate for modern society. They had, as he saw it, the ability to regulate the internal and often hidden motivations and thoughts of individuals, the first signals of their failed socialization as well as critical elements in their ultimate redemption.[22] Yet he found himself unable to explain how these controls worked. The only form of regulation for which he could account was that which occurred overtly and directly through the application of sanctions.[23]

Ross, it seems, recognized the need for a theory of social control that was consistent with emerging ideas of deviance. What eluded him, however, was an understanding of the psychological mechanism that explained how control operated internally within individuals. Within a decade, however, another early American sociologist, Charles Horton Cooley, provided the missing explanation. Like Ross, Cooley was troubled by America's transition to an urban, industrialized nation. Yet he was less concerned than was Ross about the specter of social disruption. In his notion of the social self, he had identified the internal psychological element that could contain any such threats. According to Cooley, the social self emerged spontaneously in social interaction as those so engaged came to view themselves from a common and shared perspective. It led individuals to adopt attitudes and patterns of behavior that accorded with the norms of the social group to which they belonged.

For Cooley, then, social order was not problematic. It was the natural outcome of social interaction.[24] Writing in the last decade of the nineteenth century, Ross attempted but ultimately failed to articulate a theory of social control to match an emerging understanding of deviance. Early in the next century, Cooley had devised just such a theory.

A major impact of this new understanding of deviance was to extend the task of social control beyond the coercive agencies of society to its educational and medical institutions. In fact, the ultimate effect of this shift in thinking was to attenuate the distinction between correction on the one hand and education and treatment on the other. Between the late 1880s and mid-1930s, for example, specialists in the emerging field of classroom management sought to use the schools to instill children with internal mechanisms of self-discipline. As they saw it, the task of public education was to transform children from beings whose behavior was externally controlled into individuals who directed their own conduct. Individuals should act correctly because that was the right thing to do, not because they were forced. Self-control was the mechanism within the individual that brought about this right conduct voluntarily.[25] Writing in 1893, Emerson White likened self-control to the springs and wheels of a clock and spoke of it as constituting an "inner impulse."[26]

These classroom management specialists saw programs of student government as an especially effective means of shifting the disciplinary locus from external authority to self-control and the motivation from coercion to voluntarism. One of the most elaborate of these early efforts was the student government program established in 1915 at Washington Junior High School in Rochester, New York. Under this program, the school was divided into fifty-two homerooms composed of thirty-five students each. Each homeroom elected five class officers: a president who served as presiding officer, a vice-president who was the homeroom's business manager, a secretary-treasurer or usher who assisted school visitors, and a deputy in charge of homeroom discipline. Each of these homeroom officers belonged, in turn, to a group made up of his or her counterparts throughout the school, which was under the direction of a faculty advisor. The vice-presidents' group, for example, was in charge of the monthly inspection of the building for fire and sanitary hazards, while the secretary-treasurers' group was responsible for operating the student savings account program. In addition, there were four schoolwide committees composed of upper-grade students: a lunch committee, a committee of messengers, a committee of school traffic deputies, and a marshals' committee. The marshals' committee was responsible for guarding against thefts in the school cloakrooms. To improve its effectiveness, it was a secret society whose members were unknown to other students. Participating in such a program, according to the school's administration, would teach children to take responsibility for their own conduct. They would learn to regulate their behavior voluntarily without external coercion. They would be prepared to assume the kind of self-direction required of citizens in a democratic society.[27]

Similarly, medical specialists embarked upon the work of social control. In 1909, for example, a group of prominent physicians and laypersons, including Clifford Beers, Adolph Meyer, and William Welch, established the National Committee for Mental Hygiene in an attempt to use medical knowledge, particularly psychological and psychiatric research, for the solution of current social problems.[28] One of the first problems that the Committee directed its attention to was that of juvenile delinquency. In 1912, Thomas Salmon, the Committee's medical director, used a portion of the proceeds of a $50,000 grant from the philanthropist Henry Phipps to conduct a series of surveys of institutionalized dependent and delinquent children.[29]

Ten years later, in 1922, the National Committee, with the financial support of the Commonwealth Fund, undertook a four-pronged child guidance demonstration project to prevent juvenile delinquency. First, the Bureau of Children's Guidance was established at the New York School of Social Work. The Bureau's charge was to train psychiatric social workers and visiting teachers and to place visiting teachers in several New York City public schools where they would identify behavior-disordered students. Second, the Division on the Prevention of Delinquency was created within the Committee with the responsibility of establishing child guidance clinics in several cities. Affiliated with a juvenile court, hospital, or public school, these clinics were designed to assist local communities in addressing the behavior problems of children. Third, the Committee on Visiting Teachers was created to place and support visiting teachers in public schools throughout the country. And finally, the Joint Committee on Methods of Preventing Delinquency was established to coordinate and publicize the work of the project.[30]

The mental hygiene movement was, as it turns out, one of the first instances of what would be the increasing participation during the next half-century of the medical community in the regulation of deviance. Such involvement is often referred to as the *medicalization of deviance*. That is, individual and social problems that had been seen as nonmedical are redefined using medical discourse and treated employing medical procedures. In time, psychiatrists, psychologists, and even ordinary physicians would assume roles once monopolized by the police and other criminologists. They would bring such techniques as group counseling, psychosurgery, behavior modification, and drug therapy to the work of penology. Under their influence, crime would come to be seen as a sickness. Criminals and other deviants, then, were not responsible for their behavior. They were individuals whose failed socialization was the result of organic or psychological defects that rendered them sick and required a therapeutic regimen if they were to be reintegrated into society.[31]

The most significant impact of this demonstration project for our purposes was that it brought this medical effort to combat deviance into the schools. The affiliation of child guidance clinics with the public schools, as was done in the Minneapolis demonstration project, provided entry into the schools for those concerned with the identification and management of childhood behavior problems. Placing visiting teachers in the schools would, in the short term, involve educators in this effort. In time, it would prepare the way for the emergence of guidance counseling and school psychology as regular school functions. The efforts of the promoters of child guidance, when taken together with those of other like-minded reformers, would serve in the long run to expand the work of the schools to include the treatment of an ever-growing category of childhood deviance, including emotional disturbance, social maladjustment, and learning disabilities.[32] Their efforts, in other words, would serve to blur what has traditionally differentiated the tasks of education, therapy, and criminology.

One such body of reformers was the National Conference on the Education of Backward, Truant, and Delinquent Children. Spanning the years 1904 to 1921, the Conference, a forerunner of the National Conference of Social Work, was one of the first groups to make the case for expanding the role of the school to that of accommodating children with learning difficulties.

IV.

Turn-of-the-century American educators used the term *backward* to refer to a diverse lot of children who were not adjusting to the academic and social demands of the public schools. Sometimes, they used the term as a synonym for *mental deficiency*. More often, however, they employed the concept of backwardness to talk about intellectually normal children whose school failure was the result of environmental deficits or cognitive dysfunctions of uncertain origin.[33] It was these children who would ultimately become the learning disabled and at-risk students whom I shall consider in this volume.

Speaking at the seventh annual Conference on the Education of Backward, Truant, and Delinquent Children in 1910, Howard McQueary of Soldan High School in St. Louis noted that the salient feature of backward children was that they were intellectually normal:

> By "backwardness," we refer more to school attainments than
> to mental status, that is our emphasis is upon failure to make
> regular progress in grades with the average group of chil-
> dren, or unbalanced accomplishments. This may be due to a
> great many causes, such as late entrance into school; the
> lockstep in promotion; frequent transfer from school to
> school, or from teacher to teacher, the presence of physical
> defects, and sickness causing irregular attendance; poor
> teaching; and home indulgence; in addition to mental in-
> capacity or delayed maturity; so that there may be a general
> all-round retardation; or backwardness may be manifest only
> in some particular subject or study.[34]

Educators who were interested in the plight of these children advanced numerous explanations for backwardness.
Some believed that the problem was environmental. In his
introduction to Henry Goddard's text on backward children,
Paul Hanus noted that these were children "who for some
cause, local, environmental, physical, or somewhat mental are
slow, dull and cannot progress at the rate that our ordinary
school curriculum presupposes."[35] At the 1909 meeting of the
Conference on the Education of Backward, Truant, and Delinquent Children, Florence McNeal identified eighteen categories of backwardness, over half of which could be attributed to
environmental or social causes. Included among the backward,
she noted, were children who could not speak English, had
poor self concepts, had unsatisfactory school attendance, had
weak study skills, or could not complete their required school
work.[36]

   William Bodine, Superintendent of Compulsory Education
for the Chicago Public Schools, attributed increases in backwardness in his address to the 1905 meeting of the Conference
to what he saw as the unwholesome characteristics of modern
urban life. There was, Bodine stated, the problem of unre-
stricted immigration, which was allowing the entry into the
country of "illiterates" and others who would make "undesirable citizens." Such individuals, he believed, would not recognize the need to send their children to school. Another fac-
tor in the increasing incidence of backwardness, Bodine
believed, was the ease with which people could marry and have

children. "We forget that there is no uniform marriage law to stop the marriage of the feeble-minded, epileptics, consumptives, habitual drunkards, and school girls in short dresses who play with fate to the tune of the wedding march."

There were, Bodine argued, other aspects of modern urban life that were responsible for backwardness. They included the ready access that children living in the city had to liquor, tobacco, cocaine, and opium, the countless opportunities they had to engage in gambling, and the confinement brought about by apartment living. Even the rise of labor unions, he believed, had contributed to increases in backwardness. Students who witnessed strikes and the other organizational efforts of incipient unions, Bodine believed, acquired a disrespect for law, which frequently led to acts of disobedience and defiance in the classroom.[37] These were conditions, Bodine pointed out, that were unknown in the nation's rural past:

> Slowly but surely, the home is passing away in the cities—the old fashioned home with its green yards and flowers, its broad porch, and comfort for child life. There are few if any neurotics among country children where they live next to nature and where they grow up into robust manhood and womanhood as nature's own.[38]

Others, however, put forth a medical explanation for the problem and attributed backwardness to brain damage. During the discussion of his paper at the 1905 Conference on the Education of Backward, Truant, and Delinquent Children, Charles Krauskopf, Secretary of the Illinois Society for Child Study, stated that this problem was the result of children's "nervous organization." What was perplexing about these children, he went on to say, was that despite the lack of any physical defect, "some portion of the brain has not developed fully."[39] A member of the audience, a Dr. Abbott, noted the difficulty brought about by the inability to actually locate the brain injury:

> When you come to the children that are backward, these children that are not right and we don't know exactly what to do, it is an extremely difficult problem. There may be no

defect apparent and still the child may suffer from these mental deficiencies to a greater or lesser degree.[40]

Writing in 1914, Barbara Morgan took a similar position. She described backward children as those exhibiting "inherent fundamental brain disturbance," a "sense defect," or a "slow rate of development."[41] And twelve years later, Annie Inskeep suggested that one of the characteristics of backwardness was word blindness, "a condition arising because of a lesion of the left or, if the patient is left-handed, the right angular gyrus or a cellular deficiency in the same region."[42]

Notwithstanding the cause of backwardness, advocates for these children believed that the schools often exacerbated the problem. At the 1905 meeting of the Conference, Nelson McLain, Superintendent of the St. Charles School for Boys, argued that backwardness could be brought on by a school curriculum that "failed to nourish the mental growth or to engage, employ and direct the physical activities of child life."[43] A year later, at the 1906 meeting, William Shearer, Superintendent of Schools in Elizabeth, New Jersey, pointed to the role that the school plays in causing backwardness:

> I think that it may be shown that the very large proportion (I can't say all) of the so-called backward children are not backward because of inherited mental or physical defects but are considered backward and made to appear backward because of the methods which we are using in our public schools.[44]

Shearer went on to claim that for many children the existing curriculum was inappropriate. "We are stuffing the coming men and women in our school with a lot of matter which is not digestible, which cannot go to build strong brains."[45] In responding to a comment by a conference participant about the ability of backward children to adjust to the demands of adult society, Shearer was even more direct in placing the responsibility on the schools. "These so-called backward children, when they get out in life, prove they were not backward but very much forward and I believe we are responsible largely for keeping them back when we should not."[46]

The membership of the Conference was dominated by administrators of state residential schools for delinquent youth. Yet they believed that the public schools should make accommodation for backward children. Placing backward children in state institutions, Krauskopf noted at the 1905 meeting of the Conference, would segregate them unnecessarily:

> The special teacher will trend away from the conventional instruction so much that the vital connection with the rest of the school system will be lost and will thus tend to prevent transfers to and from the regular classes. Quite a per cent of these slow children can be so strengthened by special instruction that they can enter the regular grade work for certain periods, if not permanently, much to their benefit and occasionally a normal child can be helped greatly by work with the special teacher. This helpful interchange can only be secured by keeping the special classes under the administrative system and making them an organic part of some school. In order to preserve this organic relationship the modifications of the curriculum and methods of instruction for the subnormal should be as small as possible, consistent with good results to the individual.[47]

V.

Exploring, as we have done, the evolution of our thinking about deviance has brought us part way toward an understanding of the development of public school programs for children with learning difficulties. It was a reasonable course of action for those who embraced a therapeutic role for the public school to accept responsibility for children who were difficult to teach. The willingness of school reformers to accommodate these students, however, does not explain why they created special schools and classes for this purpose. If we are to understand why they did so, we must look at their efforts as part of the attempt of Progressive era reformers to enhance the administrative capacity of an emerging American state—that is, those agencies and individuals in the public sphere who hold obligatory authority over others.[48]

The establishment of special schools and classes was a local effort not dissimilar to national, state-building initiatives of the day. In both instances, individuals working in incipient bureaucratic organizations sought to fashion new institutional structures to cope with the changes accompanying the nation's transition to a market economy.[49] The attempts of Presidents Roosevelt, Taft, and Wilson to reform the Interstate Commerce Commission (ICC) between 1904 and 1920 represent one such effort. Each in their own way, these three Progressive era presidents sought to increase the Commission's power to regulate the nation's railroads beyond that contained in the 1887 Interstate Commerce Act. By expanding the rate-making authority of the ICC and giving it new power to supervise the operation of railroads, they enhanced the federal executive's capacity to regulate transportation over and against that of the Congress and the courts.[50] Similarly, the creation of special schools and classes offered a bureaucratic strategy to enable urban school systems to adjust their operations to increasing enrollments.[51]

School managers—my term for those educational administrators, board of education members, and local politicians who oversee the operation of the public schools—were not, as it turns out, the sole promoters of these reforms. Twentieth century efforts to provide for low-achieving children, not unlike many other social welfare reforms, were not simply state initiatives. Voluntary, philanthropic organizations, as I noted earlier and as we shall see in chapter four, often established these programs with public involvement occurring much later in response to inadequacies, unanticipated or otherwise, in these initial private efforts.

Lester Salamon has referred to this public-private interplay as third-party government. As Salamon sees it, historical accounts of the development of social welfare have concentrated their attention on the growth of public expenditures during the twentieth century. As a consequence, these investigations have tended to ignore the role of private agencies in the provision of social services. The combination of philanthropic initiatives with public funding, Salamon goes on to say, has had the effect of increasing "the role of government in promoting the general welfare without unduly enlarging the state's administrative apparatus."[52] The state-centered interpretation that I will advance in this volume, then, will take into account the role played by the interaction between the schools and private philanthropy.

VI.

In the remainder of this volume, I examine what we might think of as the first crusade for the education of at-risk students. That is, I am concerned with the events occurring between the establishment of the first public school programs for backward children at the turn of the twentieth century and the appearance of learning disabilities some sixty years later. I will explore those events in two public school systems, those of Atlanta, Georgia, and Minneapolis, Minnesota.[53] In the chapters that follow, I will be looking at both the way school managers conceptualized and talked about children with learning difficulties and the institutional arrangements that they introduced to accommodate these students. In the latter instance, I will focus my attention on the interplay between the public schools and private philanthropy. Throughout the volume, I will be concerned with exploring the contradictory purposes that appeared to guide this reform effort.

In chapter two, I examine the development of special classes for backward children in the Atlanta Public Schools between 1898 and 1924. Employing a state-centered interpretive framework, I explore the reasons why the city's school managers created special classes to accommodate these low-achieving children. In chapter three, I consider how the appearance of a medical discourse for talking about deviance influenced our understanding of childhood learning difficulties. I first examine how the research of a number of psychologists and educators from the early 1930s onward transformed the rather uncertain condition of backwardness into a full-fledged neurological impairment, minimal brain injury. I then explore the efforts of parents of low-achieving children to popularize, under the rubric of learning disabilities, this medical understanding of childhood learning difficulties.

Chapter four examines the role of private philanthropy to promote public school programs for learning disabled children. I will look specifically at the work of the Atlanta Junior League during the 1930s to establish a citywide clinic for the treatment of childhood speech and language problems, a facility that from the beginning provided services for children with neurological impairments. I then examine the attempts of the League after 1938 to promote the expansion of these services to the public schools, a campaign that resulted in the establishment in 1967 of Atlanta's first public school program for learning disabled children.

In chapter five, I shift my focus to Minneapolis and examine the effort of that city's public schools to accommodate children with learning difficulties. Looking at the period between 1930 and 1970, I explore the transformation of the city's remedial services into a program for learning disabled children.

The book will conclude with an epilogue that examines the emerging movement for the education of at-risk children. Appearing on the scene at the end of the decade of the 1980s, this initiative reflects the same contradictory purposes that have affected other earlier efforts on the part of school managers to accommodate children with learning difficulties. There are, I argue, indicators of an emerging sea change in our understanding of childhood learning difficulties that may enable those supporting the education of at-risk children to reconcile their conflicting goals. One such indicator has been the increasing criticism of curriculum differentiation on the part of educational researchers. A second has been the attack, beginning in the 1970s, on segregated special education. A third and final sign of this impending change has been a conceptual crisis among special educators involving the continued viability of learning disabilities as a handicapping category. Finally, I look at what the historical developments we have explored throughout this volume tell us about the current effort to educate at-risk students.

In this introductory chapter, I have established our conceptual framework for examining the evolution throughout this century of public school programs for children with learning difficulties. The strategy is two-pronged and involves an investigation of changes since the mid–eighteenth century in our understanding of deviance and an examination of the state-building efforts of American school managers. Using this strategy, we were able in the chapter to explain why turn-of-the-century school reformers came to accept responsibility for the education of children with learning difficulties, and why they selected special classes and schools as their vehicles for this purpose. In subsequent chapters, the same strategy will enable us to examine the evolution of these programs, first into an array of remedial classes for low-achieving children and ultimately into initiatives for the education of the learning disabled. Tracing the history of this reform effort will in the end provide us with a fresh vantage point for interpreting the now emerging movement for the education of at-risk children.

2

Educating Atlanta's Backward Children, 1898–1924

When mid-nineteenth-century educational reformers described the system of common schools that they envisioned, they talked about an institution that would be accessible to all children and would offer them a shared educational experience.[1] Writing in 1826, Congressman Charles Mercer of Virginia saw the common school as a key element in promoting American democracy:

> But the equality on which our institutions are founded cannot be too intimately interwoven in the habits of thinking of our youth; and it is obvious that it would be greatly promoted by their continuance together, for the longest possible period in the same schools of juvenile instruction: to sit upon the same forms; engage in the same competitions; partake of the same recreations and amusements, and pursue the same studies, in connexion with each other; under the same discipline and in obedience to the same authority.[2]

And eight years later, a report of a joint committee of the Pennsylvania Legislature argued that educating children of different social classes together could mitigate against the unfair advantage of wealth:

> Let them all fare alike in the primary schools; receive the same elementary instruction; imbibe the same republican

spirit, and be animated by a feeling of perfect equality. In after life, he who is diligent at school, will take his station accordingly, whether born to wealth or not.[3]

Yet it was not always the case that common educational experiences were provided. Throughout the nineteenth century, school reformers debated the question of whether boys and girls should be educated together or separately. While coeducation was the dominant pattern for organizing schools during this period, it was not uncommon for boys and girls to be educated separately in single-sex settings.[4] Many of the first high schools offered students several alternative programs, including a classical course devoted to the study of Latin and Greek, and an English course involving the study of modern foreign languages, higher mathematics, natural science, and such practical subjects as bookkeeping and drawing.[5] And in 1838 the Boston School Committee created a number of intermediate schools or "schools for special instruction" to accommodate children who had not acquired the basic reading skills needed for admission to the city's grammar schools but were too old to attend the primary schools.[6]

America's transition to a market economy would bring further departures from this common school ideal. Two features of this economic transformation, the creation of markets in which labor was bought and sold for wages and industrialization, would dramatically increase school attendance.[7] Between 1880 and 1920, the elementary and secondary school population would virtually double from almost ten million children to over twenty-one million.[8] Historians, as it turns out, are divided about why this occurred. Some have embraced a functionalist account that attributes this increase to the demands of an industrial economy for more skilled workers. Others argue that societal changes associated with a market economy, particularly an increasing living standard, both allowed children to attend school longer and engendered fears about the risks associated with leaving school for the workplace. And still others explain this enrollment increase in terms of labor force changes that enhanced the credentialing value of educational achievement for job mobility.[9] What is not disputed, however, is that this enrollment growth brought an increasingly diverse population into the schools. And to cope with that diversity, schools initiated various forms of curriculum differentiation. One type of differentiation was vocational education.[10] A second, and the one that will occupy our attention in this chapter, was the establishment of special classes for backward and mentally retarded children.

II.

The half-century following the close of the Civil War was a period of significant population growth for the city of Atlanta. In 1870 Atlanta had a population of 21,789. Ten years later, the population had increased seventy-two percent to 37,409. An even higher growth rate during the following decade gave the city a population of 65,533 in 1890. By 1920 Atlanta's population had reached 200,616 inhabitants.[11]

During this period, Atlanta enjoyed significant economic expansion. Between 1870 and 1900, the city's capital investment increased from about a half-million to sixteen million dollars. In 1870 Atlanta contributed about three percent of Georgia's manufacturing output. By 1919 that amount had grown to eighteen percent. By 1920 the city had become a major manufacturing center in the South with about thirty percent of its male workers employed in manufacturing and mechanical industries.[12]

Atlanta inaugurated its system of public schooling amid this growth. During January and February 1872, the city opened four public schools for its white children, two grammar schools, Boys High School, and Girls High School. Within a month, the city had to open two more grammar schools to accommodate the demands for additional classroom space. At the same time, Atlanta established a system of separate grammar schools for the city's black children by assuming responsibility for two existing schools for blacks, one operated by the Freedmen's Bureau and the other by the American Missionary Society. [13] In the course of the next half-century, the city school system would expand. By 1921 Atlanta operated forty-four grammar schools and four high schools for its white children, and fifteen grammar schools for its black children.[14]

Growth was, however, not an unreserved success. Neither the city's infrastructure nor the municipal services that it offered was adequate for the emerging urban center that Atlanta was becoming. The city, according to Darlene Roth, was in virtual disrepair:

> City services were grossly inadequate: there were not enough utilities, parks, streets, sewers, or schools. According to one estimate, at least a third of the population was not served by sewers, and more than half of the residential streets were not paved. Epidemics of dyptheria and typhoid were common, and the number of tuberculosis cases was reaching an all time high. There was a high death rate in the city, a high crime rate, and a high rate of juvenile delinquency and vagrancy. In 1905, more children were arrested for disturbing the peace in Atlanta than anywhere else in the United States.[15]

Similarly, the city's schools suffered from a deteriorating physical plant. A 1921 survey of Atlanta's schools reported that twenty-one of the city's white grammar schools, three of its high schools, and twelve of its black grammar schools were housed in buildings that were judged to be "inferior" and in all likelihood beyond repair.[16]

It was during the first two decades of the twentieth century, amid the city's population growth and economic expansion, that Atlanta's school managers would begin to grapple with the problems of low-achieving children. Addressing the city's Board of Education at its January 1898 meeting, Superintendent William F. Slaton called for the adoption of a regulation to "prevent children of dull minds and weak intellects from remaining 3 or 4 years in the same grade." Their presence, Slaton stated, was leading "to the annoyance of the teacher and detriment of the grade."[17]

The first concrete proposal for addressing this problem was not made, however, until September 1908. Two teachers, a Miss Mitchell and a Miss Dunlap, suggested to the Board of

Education that students "whose conduct and lessons for the day are satisfactory" be allowed to leave school at 1 P.M. while "slow and backward pupils and those with unprepared lessons" be held to 2 P.M., thereby giving them additional time to complete their work. Neither Superintendent William M. Slaton who had succeeded his father in that job the year before, nor Assistant Superintendent Leonidas Landrum was willing to accept the recommendation. Slaton offered no real reason for his decision, but did comment that the proposal "would result in injury to all."[18]

The Board of Education, however, was more sympathetic to the idea. It asked the Committee on Schools and Teachers to study the matter and to a make report. Two months later, in November, the Board accepted this committee's recommendation to dismiss the first grade at 1 P.M. daily. First-grade teachers would then be freed from their classroom responsibilities and instead would work with "backward children" in the other grades until the regular dismissal time.[19]

Judging by his rhetoric, Slaton was not opposed to all measures for dealing with difficult to teach children.[20] In 1911 he urged the Board to provide some assistance to "backward children." And a year later, Slaton spoke to the Board about the need to establish special classes for delinquent children: "It is not just that fifty or sixty children in a class should be retarded by two or three refractory members whose parents through weakness or ignorance have not taught and trained them at home to obey school authority."[21]

Although the Board that year did open up a class for deaf children at Ashby Street School and appointed a teacher to work with tubercular children confined to the city's Battle Hill Sanitorium, it was not willing to establish special classes for low-achieving children."[22] Two years later, in December 1914, the Board, which had recently elected as its president Robert Guinn, a proponent of school reform, authorized that several vacation schools be established the following summer. Such schools, the Board hoped, would allow students who had failed during the regular year to make up their work and would allow abler children to advance more rapidly.[23] The vacation schools, however, did not seem to address the difficulties of all children with learning problems. In a report to the Board after the conclusion of its first session in June 1915, the administrators of the vacation schools, Laura Smith and Ora Stamps, noted the problem created by "children whose mentality is deficient and whose presence in the school room hinders the instruction of normal children." They called on the Board to establish special classes for these children. Landrum, who had replaced Slaton as superintendent that month, supported the proposal and the Board approved.[24]

Within several weeks, the city's first special class for mentally deficient white children was opened at Fair Street School.[25] At the end of its first month of operation, the principal, Gussie Brenner, reported to the Board of Education on the progress of the program. She noted that the class was instilling "backward children" with self-respect, helping those whose retardation was improvable to return to their regular grade, and preparing the "worst cases" to be self-sufficient.

Evidently impressed with her report, the Board authorized the establishment of two more special classes for white children by the end of the year, one at Boulevard Street School and the other at Lee Street School.[26] By 1920 the city would have seven special classes in its white grammar schools and, for a short time, two special classes in its black grammar schools.[27]

A year later, in June 1916, Laura Smith, Primary Supervisor and administrator of the special classes, reported to the Board of Education on the operation of this new program. Most of her report was devoted to day-to-day administrative matters, including teacher appointments and salaries, and the expansion of the program to three more schools, Luckie Street, Ashby Street, and Fraser Street schools. Toward the end of her report, she noted the presence in the city's schools of children who were "over the age for their grade" and who were not appropriate candidates for the special classes. "These children," she pointed out, "are not mental defectives. Most of them are retarded because of lack of opportunity or illness." She went on to argue that these children represented the city's "most serious loss" because they were likely to become disheartened over their lack of progress and leave school. Smith recommended the establishment of an ungraded class where these students could be placed temporarily until they were able with the help of special teachers "to make their grades more rapidly" and thus catch up with children in the regular classroom.[28]

The following year, two ungraded classes were established, one at Boulevard Street School and the other at English Avenue School. At Boulevard, twenty-two over-age students were taken from other grades and assigned to one teacher who would work with them until they could perform at grade level and be returned to their regular classes. At English Avenue, the ungraded class was staffed by two teachers who would work with students in those areas in which they were having difficulties.[29] During the next four years, the ungraded program was expanded throughout the city until by 1922 there were ungraded classes in fourteen grammar schools. In 1924 the program was expanded to the secondary level with the establishment of two ungraded classes at Hoke Smith Junior High School.[30]

The ungraded classes were, however, a short-lived innovation. In 1923 a number of ungraded classes were renamed "adjustment" classes and given a new function. They were to serve, as the *Atlanta Constitution* reported, students who had become "repeaters." These were students "who are not handicapped in any way, but who for sufficient reasons have become temporarily misfits in the school program." With individualized instruction in reading, arithmetic, and other subjects, it was hoped that these children would "soon take their places among the boys and girls of the same mental capacity."[31]

The adjustment class was a source of pride for Superintendent Willis Sutton. In his 1924 annual report to the Board of Education, he referred to the adjustment class as a "great achievement" in Atlanta's effort to reduce its public schools' failure rate.[32] Two years later, however, a shortage of funds led the Board of Education to make a number of cutbacks including the elimination of the adjustment classes. The following year, the city's special classes were redesignated as ungraded classes, and for the remainder of the decade were Atlanta's sole program for children with learning difficulties.[33]

III.

Atlanta, as I have already suggested, was not alone in trying to accommodate a diverse array of difficult to teach children. Similar programs appeared at roughly the same time in urban school systems throughout the nation. In his 1873 report to the Detroit Board of Education, Superintendent Duane Doty noted that the existence of a number of "bad boys whose presence in the regular schools works harm" requires the establishment of an ungraded school.[34] The Board, however, did not act on Doty's recommendation. Nine years later, in 1882, the Michigan Legislature passed a compulsory attendance law, which included a provision allowing cities with a population of at least five thousand to establish ungraded schools for students who were "habitual truants" and those who were "incorrigible, vicious, or immoral in conduct." In response to this legislation, the Detroit Board of Education established ungraded classes at four of the city's elementary schools and soon thereafter opened a centrally located ungraded school.[35]

Ungraded schools were designed primarily for children whom school authorities found troublesome to manage. There were, however, as was the case in Atlanta, other children who posed problems for the regular classroom. To provide for these children, the Detroit school managers established other programs, including a class for deaf children in 1898 and a special class for so-called backward children in 1901.[36] Despite the existence of these different programs, the city had difficulty in correctly identifying and placing its exceptional students. In 1906 Superintendent Wales Martindale remarked how difficult it was to classify so-called backward children. Once the least able of these children had been identified, he noted, there was "no strong line of demarcation" among those remaining. They could be children whose development had been delayed or children who did not respond well to conventional instructional strategies.[37] The following year, Martindale urged the Board to make this differentiation:

A more definite line of demarcation must be drawn between those low grade imbeciles, known as backward, and those of

higher mentality, also known as backward, who are elim-
inated from the regular grade. The low grade cases and those
bordering on low grade must be separated from those children of possibly less than normal mentality, who are also
known as backward, because they are unable to advance in
one or more of the regular subjects. If this is not done, the
parents of the latter class will finally refuse to send their
children to these rooms and who can say that they will not be
justified.[38]

Advocating this division among difficult to teach children
was, it seems, easier than actually achieving it. A 1908 survey
of seven of the city's schools noted that children were referred
to ungraded programs not just because of recalcitrance but also
because of backwardness.[39] During the next ten or so years, the
city school managers initiated a number of efforts to achieve
this differentiation. In 1910 both the President of the Board of
Education, Charles Kahn, and Superintendent Martindale called for the exclusion of the most severely retarded children
from the public schools and the creation of a state institution
to care for them. The following year, the Board created a child
study committee and a psychological clinic to evaluate and
place children in special education and authorized the use of
the Binet test to establish the mental age of these children. By
1914 Detroit had added to its special education services classes
for blind, orthopedically handicapped, and speech impaired
children, and preparatory classes for intellectually normal
children who were experiencing academic difficulties.[40]

New York City established its first ungraded class in
1899.[41] The city school managers, like their counterparts in
Atlanta and Detroit, soon discovered the diverse array of children who found their way into this class. In a 1903 report to the
Board of Education, Associate Superintendent Edward
Stevens noted that the city's nine ungraded classes enrolled
not only children who belonged permanently in a special class
but those who could with assistance ultimately return to their
regular grade and those who were discipline problems.[42] As a
consequence, the city established during the next four years a
number of other special classes. Ungraded classes were to be

reserved for mentally retarded children. Special C classes were designed to teach English to non-English speaking and immigrant children. Special D classes were for adolescents who had fallen behind in their academic work. And Special E classes enrolled a variety of children who needed to catch up to their peers in regular classes or to move ahead more quickly. Among these students were children who were "truants and incorrigibles" and those who were "dull, backward pupils."[43]

IV.

As I noted in the last chapter, it was clearly not happenstance that accounted for the establishment of special classes in urban school systems throughout the country during the first three decades of the twentieth century. The appearance of these classes can be explained, at least in part, by the willingness of school managers to see deviance as an educational problem. Yet such an intellectual transformation does not tell the entire story. We also need to consider how the introduction of special classes provided these school managers with new administrative capacities. We need, in other words, to look at how the establishment of these classes advanced the state-building efforts of these educational officials.

During the early years of the twentieth-century, Atlanta's school system undertook a number of initiatives to expand and differentiate its program. In his 1898 and 1899 annual reports, Superintendent William F. Slaton called on the Board of Education to introduce vocational education into the city high schools to meet the needs of students who, as he put it, "are bread-winners early in life and subsequently heads of families."[44] And during May 1899, the Board received proposals urging it to introduce physical education into the curriculum and to establish kindergarten classes in several of the city schools.[45] Within the next three years, Atlanta introduced courses in shop work, business, and technology at Boys' High School and created a new administrative position, that of Director of Manual Training.[46] For Atlanta's school managers, the establishment of special classes was one phase of this larger effort at differentiation. As a 1928 Board of Education publication noted:

> There must be night schools for special needs, "opportunity schools" for grown-ups whose education has been neglected, technical training in various lines. There are high schools for boys and girls offering academic courses; a technical high school for boys; a commercial high school for both sexes. There are schools and classes for the deficient, classes for the deaf, classes for the blind.[47]

Contemporary educational historians, for the most part, have viewed curriculum differentiation as a bureaucratic strategy, which Progressive era school reformers embraced in response to the external pressures facing early twentieth-century urban schools. One source of this pressure, they argue, was the passage of compulsory attendance and child labor laws, which, taken together, brought into the schools not only greater numbers of children but children who were increasingly diverse in class, ethnicity, and ability. The introduction of numerous specialized courses of study, some preparatory and some terminal, enabled the schools, according to these scholars, to accommodate this larger and more heterogeneous school population.

Another commonly identified source of external pressure were business elites who wanted to use the educational system to produce the kind of work force that a market economy required. The introduction of vocational programs, as this interpretation goes, allowed the schools to channel children to their appropriate occupational roles in an industrial economy.[48]

Unfortunately, this interpretation does not help us in understanding the introduction of special classes in Atlanta. It does not seem that Atlanta's school managers established special classes in response to compulsory attendance legislation. Atlanta's first special class was established in 1915, a full year before the state passed its first compulsory attendance law. That law, however, was exceptionally weak. Children between eight and fourteen were supposed to attend school for four months a year through fourth grade. Yet, numerous groups of children, including those who were disabled, whose parents did not have the money to provide them with clothes and books, and others who were excused by local boards of education, were exempted from this attendance requirement.[49]

Even as late as 1920, when Atlanta had nine special classes in operation, Georgia had not passed legislation either requiring the education of the mentally retarded or providing financial support to those school districts that voluntarily established programs for these children.[50] The Georgia compulsory attendance law may have served over time to bring more low-achieving children into the schools, thus requiring the establishment of additional special classes. Nonetheless, this law does not seem to have been the impetus behind the creation of these classes.

Similarly, it is hard to attribute the introduction of these classes to the passage of child labor legislation. Georgia did enact legislation in 1906 and again in 1914 to restrict child labor. The 1914 bill prohibited children under fourteen and a half years of age from working unless they had completed twelve weeks of school during the previous twelve months. Children over twelve, however, were exempted from this requirement if they were self-supporting or if they had to support a widowed mother.[51] In 1920, despite the passage of this bill, Georgia was first in the nation in the number of children between ten and fifteen who were employed.[52]

There is also little evidence to support the claim that the Atlanta school managers created these classes at the behest of business elites. Atlanta's business and professional community was divided into so-called conservative and progressive factions. The conservatives were primarily bankers, corporate leaders, and professionals who looked to Clark Howell, editor of the *Atlanta Constitution*, for leadership. The progressive group included, for the most part, lawyers, real estate agents, and insurance salesmen under the leadership of Hoke Smith, publisher of the *Atlanta Journal* and at various times during this period governor of Georgia and United States senator. Although their struggles were often couched in the rhetoric of reaction versus reform, hence the labels of conservative and progressive, what these factions actually fought about much of the time was control of the city's political apparatus and ultimately control over the Georgia Democratic Party.[53]

This elite was one of the few segments of the city's population that had anything to say about special classes. Neither the city's black population nor organized labor addressed the issue.[54] Teachers, too, were virtually silent about this reform.[55] Yet, the views of the business elite were enigmatic. There were, for example, members of both factions who were opposed to educational innovations, including special classes. In June 1918, W.H. Terrell, an attorney and Board of Education member who often spoke for conservatives, testified before a special committee of the Atlanta City Council, which was then investigating the schools. He claimed that "certain innovations," which Robert Guinn was then advocating, would increase costs while actually decreasing the efficiency of the schools' operation.[56] Speaking before the same committee, another attorney, Harvey Hatcher, who was a supporter of Guinn and Chairman of the City Council's Finance Committee, attacked the special classes on the grounds of their cost. The Finance Committee had actually threatened to abolish these classes early in 1918 when Laura Smith requested a budget increase of one hundred dollars to purchase materials to introduce handwork into the special classes. It was only after Guinn intervened on Smith's behalf that the committee withdrew its threat.[57]

Atlanta's school managers had ties to, or were part of, this elite. Yet their views concerning special classes were not always predictable. School Board President Guinn was a member of the progressive faction and, as we noted earlier, a supporter of special classes. The Slatons and Leonidas Landrum tended to align themselves with the city's conservative faction.[58] But they joined with progressives in supporting special classes.

The key players in establishing Atlanta's special and ungraded classes, and perhaps special classes elsewhere, were not external interest groups or classes. The support for this innovation, instead, came from school managers themselves, who saw these classes as providing them with new administrative capabilities to resolve immediate problems they faced. These managers, then, were acting at their own behest to augment the capacities of the sector of the state in which they worked.

Special and ungraded classes aided the city's school managers as they confronted a number of problems. First, these classes seemed to offer school administrators a way to maintain their commitment to the common school ideal of accessibility in the face of enrollment growth. The Atlanta school managers, not unlike their counterparts in other cities, frequently voiced their belief that public schooling should be available to all children. In his 1911 annual report to the Board of Education, Superintendent William M. Slaton echoed the sentiments of mid-nineteenth-century school reformers in calling for the education of all city youth on the grounds that "ignorance and the lack of moral training is the greatest curse of mankind."[59] Two years later, Board of Education President Robert Guinn called for a high school education of all of Atlanta's children in order to ensure that they reach "the highest efficiency of which they are able."[60]

Achieving this accessibility was, however, always problematic. From its first day of operation, Atlanta never provided enough classrooms for all the children who wished to attend. Double sessions and class sizes in excess of sixty children were a common feature of the city schools.[61] Exacerbating this persistent overcrowding was the enrollment growth that occurred in the early years of the twentieth century. Between 1898 and 1915, the Atlanta white grammar school population grew from 13,254 to 21,190 students, an increase of sixty-seven percent.[62]

It was evidently burdensome accommodating some of these children. At its October 1914 meeting, the Board of Education received a letter from J.E. Ellis, a teacher at Grant Park School, concerning one of her students, who had, as she put it, an "epileptic fit." According to the letter, Grant Park's Principal, Mrs. W.P. Davis, would not allow the child to return to school "because the presence of the child was liable to cause distraction in the exercise of the school." At the same meeting, the Board also considered a letter from Belle Simpson, the teacher of the deaf at Ashby Street School, requesting the removal of one Herbert Manning: "He disturbs the class by doing many unusual and unexpected things and continuously distracts the attention of the class and the work of the teacher." Voting to remove both children from the schools, Board members stated that incidences such as these indicated that teachers faced a problem in accommodating certain "deficient and disabled children." At the suggestion of Guinn and two other members, a committee was appointed to study the problem, and the following month it proposed the introduction of vacation schools.[63]

Establishing first vacation schools and then special and ungraded classes offered a means whereby the city schools could remain accessible as the student population became larger and more diverse. Although it was ultimately necessary to segregate low-achieving children in special classes, the schools were still able to remain open to them. In creating these classes, however, Atlanta school managers were not just reacting to a need to make classrooms more manageable. They were initiating a reform that they believed would allow them, despite changing conditions, to remain true to the nation's common school ideal.[64]

Second, establishing special and ungraded classes served to enhance the professional status and advance the political agendas of Atlanta school officials.[65] I have already noted that school managers throughout the nation, not just those in Atlanta, were advocating the establishment of special classes during the years around the turn of the twentieth century. Their appeals to expand the school program by introducing special classes and other forms of curriculum differentiation were one phase of a larger effort during this period by an emerging corps of school administrators to legitimate the existence of their profession. By extolling the virtue of such bureaucratic solutions as special classes, these administrators were in effect creating an ideology celebrating technical expertise that could justify their standing as a distinct professional specialty within the schools.[66] New programs, such as special classes and vocational education, provided the symbolic trappings of incipient professionalism.[67] Promoting special classes, however, served more than an ideological function. Once school systems introduced special classes, they then had to go out and hire teachers who had expertise in educating low-achieving children. And having such teachers in their employ required these school systems to hire specialized administrative personnel as supervisors. These appeals for special classes not only legitimated school administration as a profession. They actually built the profession.[68]

William M. Slaton used the issue of special classes to solidify his professional standing by linking himself with leading educators in other cities. On at least two occasions, Slaton, as a means of spurring on reform in Atlanta, held up to the Board of Education examples of cities that had established special classes. In January 1912 he called on the Board to establish special classes for delinquent children on the grounds that these classes were to be found in the "leading cities of the United States." And two months later upon returning from a meeting of the Department of Superintendence of the National Education Association in St. Louis, he informed the Board that this city, unlike Atlanta, provided special classes for deaf, mentally defective, and delinquent children.[69]

Implicit in Slaton's remarks on both occasions was the message that if Atlanta wanted to become a progressive city, it too would have to establish special classes. Slaton's urgings were not unlike those of other similarly placed professionals in other spheres of the state who were advancing reform. Just as these individuals looked to their counterparts in other cities for innovations—say to reformers in New York City for the idea of the municipal research bureau, or to those in Galveston, Texas, for the idea of the commission form of government—so did Slaton look to school managers in St. Louis for the idea of the special class.[70]

For Robert Guinn, the promotion of special classes served to promote his political goals. Guinn came to the Board of Education as a political rival, in the Georgia Democratic Party, of the Slaton family, particularly Governor John Slaton, Superintendent William M. Slaton's brother. Not unexpectedly, then, Guinn saw the superintendent as the main obstacle to the introduction of the reforms he so favored. Almost immediately upon joining the Board in 1914, Guinn set out to embarrass the superintendent by calling for an outside survey of the city's schools. Going further, he arranged with M.L. Brittain,

State Superintendent of Public Instruction, to have the State Supervisor of Rural Schools, Celeste Parrish, who was a former student of John Dewey at the University of Chicago and a proponent of curriculum differentiation, conduct the study. Slaton in fact objected to the study on the grounds that "the board could not guard itself against wild statements and prejudices which might enter into a survey prepared by Commissioner Guinn."[71]

In her study, which took two weeks and included visits to approximately one-quarter of the city's white grammar schools and to Girls' High School, Parrish found little to approve of in Atlanta. She was particularly critical of the curriculum, because it lacked the kind of connection between the school program and the demands of adult life that she believed typified the best of Progressivism:

> In all the cities which have reached a high grade of educational efficiency, there is a distinct attempt to relate the work of the schools to the experience of the children, and to the social and industrial life of the city. The Atlanta course of study has been static for so many years that the city has outgrown it.[72]

What was needed, according to Parrish's way of thinking, was a differentiated curriculum. She recommended the introduction of manual training and home economics in the grammar and secondary schools, and the establishment of a kindergarten program. For low-achieving and troublesome children, she suggested that Atlanta follow the example of other cities and establish vocational schools and special classes.[73]

Not satisfied with simply exposing the weaknesses of the Atlanta schools under Slaton's leadership, Guinn urged the Board not to renew the superintendent's contract when it expired in June 1915. The city, Guinn argued, needed a superintendent with "progressive ideas" and "executive ability," qualities that he believed Slaton did not possess. Slaton, however, challenged Guinn's charge. Citing his support of numerous innovations in the city's schools, Slaton noted his commitment to reform:

On my recommendation and advocacy, the department of medical inspection was added to the schools. Was that progressive? On my recommendation the Normal Training School was established to manufacture our own teachers out of own house material. Was that progressive?[74]

Guinn, however, prevailed and was able to muster a nine to three majority vote of the Board of Education to remove Slaton. Guinn's choice to replace Slaton was State Superintendent Brittain, who like Parrish had attended the University of Chicago and held similarly Progressive views. Unable to convince Brittain to leave his elective office to come to Atlanta, Guinn arranged to have Landrum appointed as superintendent and then persuaded Landrum to appoint another former University of Chicago student, Joseph Wardlaw, Dean of the Faculty of the State Normal School in Athens, as assistant superintendent. In 1917, after Landrum completed one term, the Board replaced him with Wardlaw and then went on to create a new position for Landrum, that of business manager.[75]

Under Landrum and Wardlaw, Guinn was able to establish the city's first special classes. Creating special classes, then, went a long way toward augmenting the administrative capacities of the Atlanta public schools. These classes provided a mechanism through which the city's schools could remain accessible in the face of a changing school population. And promoting these classes and other forms of curriculum differentiation served, at least temporarily, to advance the career and political goals of Atlanta school managers.

V.

There was, at least initially, no distinct curriculum for Atlanta's special and ungraded classes. Nonetheless, the instruction offered children in these settings was different from what was provided in the city's regular elementary classrooms. A 1928 newspaper account of the city's special education program noted that low-achieving children were given "daily lessons in all elementary book work subjects." The task of the teacher, according to the article, was to modify the activities of the regular classroom so that they were more "concrete and practical" and thus more in accord with these childrens' abilities.

The article then went on to describe two students enrolled in Atlanta's ungraded classes, the designation used after 1923 to refer to what earlier had been its special and adjustment classes. One child, a boy, was unable to do the work of his fourth grade class and exhibited "atrocious" behavior. In the ungraded class, he was not only given work in reading, arithmetic, and geography, he was also involved in a number of practical activities, such as repairing toys for the Junior Red Cross and weaving a rug for his mother's Christmas present. "Since his placement," according to the article, "he has not been absent, nor would he think of leaving his happy schoolroom where his interest is stimulated along 'doing lines.'" A second student, a girl, did not complete grammar school until she was fourteen. Assigned to the ungraded class at Thomson Junior High School, she completed three years of "fine work" and was sent to Commercial High School to study home economics. "This girl, who could not master the regular course of study," the account concluded, "has been salvaged for society by special education."[76]

Organizing a program around everyday activities was, it seems, a common feature of these first special or ungraded classes. In describing the need for arithmetic instruction, the Detroit 1926 special class curriculum noted that the needs of citizens in this area are "very simple," involving such skills as buying, selling, and making change. Instruction for the mentally retarded, according to this guide, "should be kept within the demands ordinarily made upon the individual in a community." Similarly, reading skills were developed by drilling students with flash cards containing the messages found on common signs posted throughout the city.[77] The majority of instructional time in geography in the Detroit special classes was devoted to a study of the city itself. The curriculum guide defended this decision on the following grounds:

It should be remembered that most of these boys and girls will spend their lives in or near Detroit, for the mentally retarded as a rule are more apt to remain in the community where they are educated than is the normal child, and if they are properly educated for life in the home community, they will have little occasion to move away. The attempt is not made in the education of the mentally retarded to prepare them to cope successfully with all the problems that may arise in the life of the normal child, but rather to make it possible for them in their own home community to engage successfully in unskilled labor and to live happily in the humbler social group.[78]

In San Francisco, special class teachers were told to select reading books for their students "to correlate with school and home activities." And in Minneapolis, the special class curriculum was composed of units for each season of the year that examined such everyday needs as clothing, shelter, transportation, and recreation, to name but a few.[79]

Ultimately this effort to render the curriculum more practical resulted in a distinct course of study. In 1938 a group of Atlanta teachers developed a guidebook of suggested units for its junior high school ungraded classes. The emphasis, not unlike courses of study elsewhere, was on daily life activities. Students spent two periods a day working on integrated units, involving social studies, English, and spelling that explored such issues as shelter, conservation, transportation, and vocations. They then spent a period each in mathematics, practical science, handicraft, shop, home economics, and physical education or music.[80] In the vocations unit, which was designed to instill children with the "desire to be gainfully employed," students were encouraged to explore the possibility of entering such occupations as poultry raising, furniture repair, masonry, telegraph delivery, package wrapping, and assembly line work in meat packing plants, cotton mills, and clothing factories. The handicraft period was to involve students in making projects that were of a "vocational nature." It was hoped that these activities would teach these children to construct "attractive, salable articles," including end tables, fruit and flower baskets, whisk brooms, chairs, luncheon mats, and sweaters.[81] Like the Detroit special classes, those in Atlanta appear to have been dedicated to channeling mentally retarded children into unskilled lines of work.

VI.

Establishing special classes did open Atlanta schools to a diverse group of difficult to teach children. Between 1921 and 1923, twenty-two of the approximately one hundred twenty-five children in the city's special classes were enrolled in Lee Street School in Atlanta's West End neighborhood.[82] Designed, as we have noted, for children with retarded mental development, the policy of the Board of Education dictated that each student referred to the special class was to be given a Binet test.[83] Yet of the eighteen children for whom cumulative school records could be located, only one had a recorded I.Q. score.[84] That student, whom I will call John Bell, had an I.Q. of 64, a score that would, according to the practice of the day, lead to a placement in a special class such as the one at Lee Street.[85]

Born in 1911, Bell entered grammar school at age six. He failed to be promoted from the first-grade, having earned an A in conduct, a C in language and composition, a D in arithmetic, and Es (failure) in reading and literature, spelling, and penmanship.[86] He repeated the first-grade two more times without success. After his second attempt in 1920, he was promoted on Superintendent William F. Dyke's recommendation, despite the fact that he earned Ds in language and composition, reading and literature, and penmanship. He then went on to repeat second-grade two times and was promoted to third-grade at age ten. He evidently had extreme difficulty in this grade and, before completing it, was placed in Lee Street's special class.

There were two children who began their school careers in the special class and whose records indicate clear reasons for that placement. One, Victoria Poor, who entered the special class at age fourteen, was almost immediately recommended for placement in Ashby Street's deaf class. The other, William Fews, entered the special class at Lee Street in 1916 at age nine, transferred to the Boulevard School special class the following year, and then left school for a period of three years. In 1921 he returned to Lee Street's special class at age fourteen, at which point his records indicate that he should be placed in a residential institution for the "feebleminded." There was a third student who began school in Lee Street's special class, but there is no indication of why he was placed there.

The remaining fourteen children were sent to the special class after having encountered problems in the regular grades. It is hard to pin down exactly what these problem were. Most of these children had repeated at least one, but often several grades before being sent to the special class. There were, however, five children who successfully passed the first- and second-grades and sometime during the subsequent year were transferred to the special class. Interestingly enough, most of these children had received good grades in both conduct and effort.

Although it is difficult to draw conclusions from cumulative records that list the grades that children received without indicating anything about what actually happened in the classroom, these grades do tell us something. Some of these students did consistently earn grades that would seem to fit individuals who were mentally deficient. Jane Richards, for example, always seemed to do poorly in her academic subjects. Although she was promoted to the second-grade, she earned only Ds in her first-grade courses in reading, spelling, history, and physiology/hygiene, and Cs in arithmetic and penmanship. She then went on to repeat the second-grade twice, failing on both occasions to be promoted. In her first attempt, she earned Es in composition, spelling, and arithmetic, while in her second, she earned Es in reading and composition. After her second failure, she was placed in the special class, where she remained for the next four years. Her record was, in fact, quite similar to that of John Bell, who, as we noted earlier, had an I.Q. of 64.

Most of the Lee Street special class children, however, received both good and poor grades, which would indicate a pattern of strengths and weaknesses that is uncharacteristic of the mentally defective. Julius Holt, for example, failed the second- and fourth-grades. Nonetheless, he had received an A in arithmetic in his first attempt at the second-grade, and a B in the same subject when he repeated the grade. Later, however, his arithmetic grades did decline. In the third-grade, he earned a C in that subject, and in the fourth a D. In the year that he failed the fourth-grade, which led him to be placed subsequently in the special class, Julius received Cs in reading and literature, spelling, history, and physiology/hygiene and Ds in composition, arithmetic, and geography. Similarly, John Wynne failed fourth-grade, which led to his placement in the special class, but received Bs in penmanship, geography, and history, and Cs in conduct, effort, and literature. His only unsatisfactory grades were Ds in reading, spelling, and arithmetic.

Lee Street's special class students were a heterogeneous group. Some, no doubt, were or at least exhibited characteristics of children with mental defects. Most, however, had a pattern of grades more commonly found among children whose low-achievement was the result of such factors as frequent absences, lack of interest, poor study habits, and inadequate parental supervision. They were, in other words, children who were difficult to teach but not necessarily mentally retarded.

Despite offering a place for a diverse array of low-achieving children, the Lee Street Special Class was not particularly effective in holding these children in school. Fourteen of the eighteen children for whom records could be located never completed the Lee Street program. Six of them left the special class after a year or two to go to work or because their parents left the city. It is not clear what happened to the other eight, since there are no entries on their cumulative records after their assignment to the special class. It appears that these children dropped out of Lee Street somewhere along the way.

Four children did complete the Lee Street class and went on to attend the special class at Thomson Junior High School. Mat Hart and Eleanor Gross completed a year at Thomson and left. The other two students, John Bell and Herbert Anderson, completed three years at Thomson. Bell, who supposedly had a 64 I.Q., achieved a mixed record. His best grades were in his vocational subjects where he earned As in metal shop, printing shop, and electric shop, a B in wood shop, and a C in drawing. His worst grades were in mathematics where he received two Cs and a D, English where he received a C and two Ds, and business practice where he earned a D. In art, science, and history, however, he earned Bs. Anderson was the only Lee Street special class student to attend high school. In 1930, at age nineteen, he entered the city's Technological High School, which offered a special industrial program for older students. There is no indication on his cumulative record as to what courses he took or whether he was ultimately graduated.

Examining what happened to children admitted to Atlanta special classes helps clarify our understanding of the purposes behind this reform. Progressive era school managers, we noted in chapter one, had conflicting goals in mind when they established special classes. They claimed, first, that these classes were designed to help students and teachers in regular classrooms pursue their work without the disruptions caused by difficult to teach children. They also claimed, however, that special classes were designed to help children with learning difficulties. They seemed unable, in other words, to decide if the schools should serve all children, particularly those with learning difficulties, or only the most able. As a consequence, they claimed at one and the same time to be pursuing both goals.

Considering what we know about the operation of Atlanta special classes, it becomes difficult to believe that this program was really created to aid children with learning problems. A curriculum that prepared students for unskilled work may have been appropriate for those who were actually mentally retarded. Our data from Lee Street, however, suggest that very few special class children were so afflicted. It is doubtful that the vocational course of study offered in the special class could help less severely impaired children return to the regular classroom. This is especially true when we consider the inability of the Lee Street Special Class to hold its students in school. Assigning them to special classes seemed to guarantee that they would drop out. Introducing special classes into public schools ostensibly committed to the ideal of common schooling, then, virtually compels them to embrace missions that are contradictory.

VII.

Although the political and professional conflicts considered in this chapter may have been unique to Atlanta, the demographic and economic transformations that led Atlanta school managers to establish special classes were probably not. The establishment of special classes was a common response of urban school administrators throughout the nation during the first thirty years of this century when confronted with the enrollment growth, which the nation's transformation to a market economy had brought. A 1931 U.S. Bureau of Education survey of sixty-eight large city school systems reported that ninety-seven percent of these cities had by the end of the decade of the 1920s established special classes for backward and mentally defective children.[87]

By the beginning of the 1930s, however, educators and others began to question whether a single undifferentiated special class could accommodate the full array of low-achieving children who were then entering the nation's schools. In its 1933 report on handicapped children, the White House Conference on Child Health and Protection noted the diversity of the population of children designated by such labels as backwardness and mental retardation. There were, according to the Conference, children with I.Q. scores up to the mid-80s who exhibited a variety of deficits in adaptive behavior. It was those children whose I.Q. scores placed them in the upper range of this group for whom public school special classes represented the most appropriate placement. There were, however, other low-achieving children who required a different type of special education. There were children who had specific disabilities in "attention, memory, perception, or language." And there were children whose disabilities were environmental in nature and were due, among other things, to illness, student-teacher conflict, or inadequate study skills. These children, according to the Conference, did not require the kind of special classes that we have described in this chapter. Rather, these children needed individualized teaching in the regular classroom or "coaching classes" to enable them to catch up with their peers.[88]

Atlanta school managers had as early as 1916 recognized the need to differentiate their special education program and had created both special and ungraded classes. A shortage of funds in 1926, however, led the city to combine these two programs and to redesignate the new setting as an ungraded class. Developments in our discourse for understanding and talking about low-achieving children during the next twenty years, however, would again bring to the fore the issue of differentiation. Of particular importance in this regard would be the emerging tendency to talk about low-achievement as a problem of brain injury or neurological dysfunction. It is to that subject that I will now turn.

3

*From Backwardness to L.D.: Medicalizing the
Discourse of Learning Difficulties*

From their inception, I have already noted, special and
ungraded classes included children who were intellectually
normal but exhibited academic and behavior problems. Uncertain about the origin of these problems, early twentieth-
century educators often attributed them to an array of environmental factors and in some cases to inexplicable
neurological dysfunctions. It was these neurological problems
that appeared most perplexing to educators of the day.

Writing in 1926, Francis Maxfield of Ohio State University
reported the case of William Kirk, a ten-year-old child from a
small town in western Pennsylvania. William exhibited adequate academic achievement and scored in the average range
on a test of mental ability. Yet he had deficits in motor co-
ordination and visual perception. Although Maxfield noted
that the child had a slight articulation problem, he was unable
to find any explanation for the child's deficits. He found no
health problems or environmental factors that would explain
the difficulties. Maxfield speculated that perhaps there was
something else involved in cognitive functioning not revealed
in intelligence test scores that accounted for William's difficulty.[1] Some three hundred miles to the west in Northfield,
Michigan, researchers at the Wayne County Training School

would spend the next two decades exploring this issue and in the process fundamentally transform our understanding of low-achievement.

II.

Established in 1927, the Wayne County Training School served children in Wayne County and the city of Detroit who were categorized in the language of the day as "high grade mental defectives with delinquent tendencies and in need of social supervision." These were children who were sent to the Training School by public school authorities, by the courts, or by social welfare agencies because they were "difficult to handle" or because their living conditions were thought to be inadequate.[2] In 1937 the Training School's Superintendent, Robert Haskell, invited two German refugees, the psychiatrist Alfred Strauss and the psychologist Heinz Werner, to join Wayne County's Research Department to continue work they had begun independently in Germany on brain-injured children.

In a paper that Strauss presented to the 1939 annual meeting of the American Association on Mental Deficiency, he described a difference that Werner and he had noticed between two groups of mentally retarded children enrolled at the Training School. The records of one group, which they had referred to as being endogenously retarded, pointed to a family history of mental deficiency. The records of the second group, which they labeled exogenously retarded, indicated no family history of retardation. But the information that the parents of this latter group supplied suggested the likelihood that these children may have at sometime in their lives received a brain injury. In addition, these children exhibited neurological signs that Strauss saw as evidence of brain injury. Such signs included involuntary rapid eye movement, paralysis of certain cranial nerves, and the Babinski phenomenon or the extension of the large toe when the sole of the foot was stimulated.

Strauss then went on to note that the experiences of these two groups of children differed at the Training School. During their stay, endogenous children showed a small increase in their I.Q. scores, while the exogenous children showed a small decrease. The endogenous children exhibited no behavioral abnormalities, while the exogenous children engaged in behavior that he described as disturbed, unrestrained, and volatile.[3]

The basis for Strauss and Werner's claim that the so-called exogenous group of children were brain damaged was their acquaintance with the work of two physicians, Henry Head, an Englishman, and Kurt Goldstein, a German, who had treated World War I veterans with gunshot wounds to the brain. Strauss, in fact, had served as an assistant to Goldstein at the University of Frankfurt Neurological Institute between 1924 and 1925.[4] Head noted that these soldiers, after undergoing surgery to repair their wounds, typically exhibited deficits in their receptive and expressive language abilities. Over time as their wounds healed, he pointed out that these defects tended to disappear. Yet these veterans never completely regained their former language abilities.[5]

Goldstein described a similar phenomenon. After surgery, the soldiers whom he treated displayed a range of behavioral abnormalities. First, they exhibited an excessive or catastrophic reaction when confronting frustrating or difficult tasks. They might approach these tasks with anger, aggression, or anxiety. Or they would in other instances approach them in a disorganized and disoriented manner. Second, they appeared to be distractible. In tasks requiring perceptual ability, they often found it difficult to attend to relevant stimuli or to distinguish the figure of a perceptual display from the background in which it was embedded. Third, these soldiers seemed unable to shift easily from one task or activity to another. They perseverated or, in other words, continued in a seemingly involuntary manner to repeat the same behavior over and over again.[6]

The children whom Strauss and Werner labeled exogenous, as it turned out, exhibited virtually the same behaviors as did Head and Goldstein's patients. Consequently, Strauss and Werner argued that these children, too, were brain-injured. Brain injury, Strauss and Werner concluded, was the cause of these children's mental deficiency.[7] In reaching this conclusion, Strauss and Werner were only offering indirect and inconclusive evidence. Goldstein, in fact, had noted that it was difficult, if not impossible, to obtain "direct proof" of the existence of a brain injury. The best investigators could hope for was to observe behavioral changes in the individual that were suggestive of brain injury. To do this, Goldstein went on to argue, researchers would have to use their skills to identify the key areas of damage to the brain that account for these changes. This was, he believed, a difficult task. Investigators, he pointed out, have to be careful so as not to be deceived by what appears obvious at first glance. They have to avoid being so committed to one explanation that they refuse to change their views in light of new evidence.[8]

Strauss and Werner were mindful of Goldstein's caveat. In a paper they presented to the 1942 annual meeting of the American Psychiatric Association in Boston, they noted that there were in fact differences between their exogenous mentally defective children and brain-injured adults. It was, they stated, "still an open question whether the concrete behavior of the brain-injured child can be directly compared to the concretism of the brain-injured adult or whether in the latter we are dealing with a deviation from a genetic trait of behavior."[9] Yet in later years Strauss, particularly, seemed to forget Goldstein's warning and his own earlier cautionary remarks.

In comparing endogenous and exogenous children on a diverse array of perceptual-motor and cognitive tasks, Strauss and Werner noted numerous differences between the seemingly two groups of children. One such experiment, which they reported in a 1930 article, involved the copying of patterns constructed from marbles placed on a mosaic board onto a second blank board. These two groups of children, Strauss and Werner argued, approached the task in quite different ways. The endogenous children employed a "global strategy" in which they constructed the patterns using one uninterrupted motion. The exogenous children, on the other hand, used an "incoherent strategy" in which they constructed the patterns unsystematically using many motions. Based on their different strategies, Strauss and Werner concluded that the mental deficiency exhibited by the two groups of children was different in nature.[10]

In a second set of experiments, Strauss and Werner had these two groups of mentally defective children perform such tasks as repeating rhythmic patterns on an electronic oscillator and identifying pictures of objects presented sequentially on flash cards. The exogenous children in both instances, Strauss and Werner reported, exhibited more perseverations or persistent repetitions than did their endogenous peers.[11]

And in another study, Werner and Doris Carrison examined the tendency of exogenous and endogenous children to bestow lifelike qualities on inanimate objects. Questioning both types of children about whether certain inanimate objects, natural events, plants, and animals were alive or dead, they concluded that brain-injured mentally defective children were more likely than hereditarily mentally defective children to attribute lifelike qualities to inanimate objects and events. This indicated, they believed, that exogenous children were more likely to engage in animistic thinking than were endogenous children.[12]

Of the approximately twenty-five studies that Strauss and Werner published comparing endogenous and exogenous children, the two that are most often cited involved an examination of figure-background relationships and a study of conceptual thinking. Writing in 1941, they reported the results of a number of tests they administered at the Training School involving figure-background relationships. In one test, children were shown nine cards containing black and white drawings of common objects that were embedded in backgrounds of either wavy and jagged lines, squares, or crosses. Using a tachistoscope, the children were exposed to each picture for one-fifth of a second. The three groups of children studied included a group with normal intelligence, one composed of the endogenously retarded, and one made up of the exogenously retarded. While the normally intelligent and the endogenous children were relatively successful in identifying the objects on the cards, the exogenous children were not. They either ignored the objects on the cards and described the backgrounds, or offered vague and often incorrect descriptions of these objects.

A second test involved the use of geometric figures constructed of large circular dots that were placed within a variety of background figures composed of small dots. Using a tachistoscope, two groups of students, one composed of hereditarily retarded children and the other of brain-injured children, were presented with a half-second exposure to each of the geometric figures. After each exposure, the children were shown three cards and asked to select the card that was most like the figure presented with the tachistoscope. One card contained only the background of the original figure. The second card contained the original background with a different geometric figure. The third card contained the original figure with a different background. While over half the exogenous children chose the card showing simply the background, only one-quarter of the endogenous children made this choice.

A third series of tests involved the use of two marble boards that contained punched holes that formed a structured background. Using one of the boards and a set of marbles, Strauss and Werner constructed a series of five marble patterns. After they constructed each pattern, the children were then asked to use the other board to copy that pattern. The copies made by the endogenous children tended to be oversimplifications of the models presented. The brain-injured children, on the other hand, tended to make changes in their copies, which indicated that they were confused by the background figures.

The results of these three tests, Strauss and Werner argued, showed that the performance of hereditarily retarded and brain-injured children on tasks involving figure-background relationships differed. The hereditarily retarded children tended to complete the tasks in approximately the same way that intellectually normal children had. The exogenous children were unable to distinguish the figure from the background. The problem, according to Strauss and Werner, was due to the inability of brain-injured children to adequately organize their perceptual field or to their inability to attend to the relevant stimuli in that field.[13]

A year later, in 1942, Strauss and Werner published their study comparing the conceptual abilities of endogenous and exogenous children. The study included three tests, two requiring the appropriate sorting of objects and one requiring the matching of pictures and objects. In the first test, fifty-six common objects, including a glass bottle, a hairpin, a small metal key, and a paper clip, to name but a few, were presented to two groups of children, one endogenous and the other exogenous. They were asked first to name the objects and then to group those that belonged together. After they completed the task, the children were asked to explain why they formed the groups they did. In a second sorting test, again involving a group of endogenous and exogenous children, a single object was placed on a table in front of the children with three objects placed directly opposite this first object. The children were asked which of the objects "goes best" with the object in front of them. The groups selected by the children in both sorting tests were of two types, combinations based on similar features or functions and combinations based on some "unessential or accidental functional relationship" among the objects. Endogenous children, for the most part, tended to make groups of the first type, while exogenous children formed those of the second type. One brain-injured child, for example, grouped a bell and a whistle together because they both sounded loud. Another exogenous child placed a picture of a bell and a ping-pong ball together because they both began with the letter *b*.

On the third test, the two groups of children were shown two pictures pasted on white cardboard, a picture of a supposedly drowning boy engulfed by waves and one of a building on fire with firemen attempting to put out the fire. Placed near the two pictures were eighty-six toy objects, including human and animal figures, toy cars and trucks, and various utensils. The children were asked to select those objects that went with each of the pictures and to place them near those pictures, and to set those objects that went with neither picture off to the side. As in the previous tests, the hereditarily retarded children selected objects that had a clear functional relationship with the pictures, while the brain-injured children selected objects whose relationships with the pictures was unclear or odd. One brain-injured child, for example, took a light bulb and placed it near the picture of the burning building. He stated that this was the bulb that blew out a fuse thereby starting the fire. Another brain-injured child placed a bar of soap near the picture of the drowning boy and stated that this was to wash the child when he came out of the water.

These three tests, Strauss and Werner argued, required children to select objects "on the basis of their belongingness either to a another object or to a pictured situation." They were, in other words, tests of the relationships between concepts. On all of the tests, the brain-injured children were more likely than the hereditarily retarded children to make uncommon groups and to group objects according to their nonessential and unimportant attributes. As part of this experiment, Strauss and Werner also administered the second and third tests to a group of intellectually normal children at University Elementary School in Ann Arbor, Michigan. They found that these normal children tended to make selections that were more similar to those of the hereditarily retarded children than to those of the brain-injured children.[14]

III.

From the first, questions were raised about Strauss and Werner's distinction between endogenous and exogenous mental deficiency. In a discussion following the presentation of one of their studies at the 1940 meeting of the American Psychiatric Association in Cincinnati, Leo Kanner commented that some may doubt the efficacy of the criteria that Strauss and Werner were using to distinguish these two supposed types of mental deficiency. He went on, however, to say that the "marked" differences between the so-called endogenous and exogenous children in their performance on the perceptual-motor and cognitive tests used by Strauss and Werner did seem to support their conclusion about the existence of two types of mental deficiency. Kanner then asked if Strauss and Werner had employed electroencephalographic examinations of the exogenous children to confirm their diagnosis of brain injury. Strauss stated that they had not, because the equipment was unavailable. He thought, however, that such studies would, if undertaken, "be very useful."[15]

Seven years later, Strauss would change his mind about the usefulness of the electroencephalograph. These studies, he pointed out, do indicate the existence of brain lesions when existent. They also, however, indicate similar pathological findings among behavior disordered children who are not in fact brain-injured, and as well among certain normal children. One could not, Strauss argued, rely totally on the electroencephalograph for making a diagnosis of brain injury. It was necessary to have other indicators, including test results similar to the ones that he and Werner had obtained, and the presence of the kind of neurological signs that were exhibited by the exogenous children at the Training School.[16]

Seymour Sarason, a Yale psychologist, was less charitable in his assessment of Strauss and Werner's work. There were, Sarason argued, problems with using children's developmental histories, as Strauss and Werner had done, to obtain evidence of brain injury. First, such histories are often based on parent reports, which were, he believed, of questionable accuracy. What an attending physician believed to be a normal birth, he thought, could appear to an expectant mother to be "the most hellish of experiences." And if reported later in such terms, it could mistakenly provide evidence of birth trauma. Second, Sarason noted that one supposed indicator of brain damage cited by Strauss and Werner, anoxia, could often have no effect on children's intellectual abilities. The existence of perinatal or postnatal anoxia in a child's developmental history was not, Sarason argued, in and for itself evidence that brain damage had occurred.

Sarason also had difficulty with the neurological signs that Strauss and Werner had cited as evidence of the presence of brain injury. The signs that they had identified, Sarason noted, were in fact indicators of damage to those descending nerve tracks, the pyramidal and extrapyramidal tracts, that transported motor impulses from the brain to the spinal cord. These signs did not, he stated, indicate damage to the area of the brain responsible for cognitive functioning. Sarason believed that the presence of these neurological signs in a mentally retarded child did not necessarily mean that the lesion responsible for the nerve track damage was also responsible for the retardation.

Finally, Sarason questioned the perceptual-motor and cognitive tests that Strauss and Werner had used to distinguish the so-called exogenous children from their endogenous peers. While these tests indicated that differences existed between these two groups of children, they were not sufficient in and for themselves without more direct evidence of pathology to prove the existence of brain injury.

The other seemingly more direct evidence of pathology that Strauss and Werner had presented—parent reports and the existence of neurological signs—was to Sarason's way of thinking suspect. "The fact," he argued, "that the exogenous cases seem to behave like some brain-injured adults cannot be considered proof that brain injury underlies 'exogenous' functioning."[17] It was difficult, he concluded, to substantiate the existence of brain injury from the kind of symptoms exhibited by Strauss and Werner's so-called exogenous children:

> The presence of major neurological signs, marked physical handicap, and intellectual incompetence—all present since birth—makes the diagnosis of diffuse brain injury a valid one. In many of these cases direct procedures have demonstrated the nature of the pathological brain condition. The exogenous child, by the very absence of major neurological symptoms or marked intellectual retardation presents a much more difficult diagnostic-etiologic problem.[18]

Interestingly enough, Goldstein, from whom Strauss and Werner had derived their brain injury hypothesis, had made virtually the same point as Sarason a decade earlier. The key problem in diagnosing brain injury, Goldstein had noted, was the failure of researchers to recognize how complex the problem was. "We have become so accustomed to regard symptoms as direct expressions of damage in a part of the nervous system that we tend to assume that, corresponding to some given damage, definite symptoms must inevitably appear."[19] Behavioral symptoms were not, Goldstein believed, such definite indicators. Rather they often represented attempts on the part of individuals to solve problems imposed on them by the environment or by an examiner in an artificial test situation:

> In this way, complete loss of a special function tends to be the outstanding symptom, and conceals the real or basic defect. On other occasions, these phenomena appear, more or less accidentally, as outstanding symptoms, which are answers elicited by specific questions presented by the examiner.[20]

Writing in 1948 on the problem of aphasia, Goldstein made a similar point. Is there, he asked, a direct connection between certain individual behavior and a particular functional disturbance such that we can view the behavior as a definite symptom of the disturbance? This was not the case with aphasia. An identical behavioral symptom could have different causes. It could be an indicator of a disturbance. Or it could just as easily be "the expression of protective mechanisms which the organism utilizes against the disastrous effect of the defect."[21]

IV.

Despite these criticisms, Strauss, whose collaboration with Werner ceased after 1945, refused to abandon his notion of exogenous brain injury. Writing in 1947 with Laura Lehtinen, he noted how one's training and theoretical orientation could affect one's conclusions about the behavioral differences that he and Werner had found among the children at the Wayne County Training School:

> It should not be overlooked, however, that there is an unavoidable personal equation resulting from the scientific training and theoretical preference of the clinician. If he prefers the psychoanalytic theory or the theory of behaviorism, if he stresses environmental factors or factors of heredity, or if he adheres to neurophysiological theories or to psychological ones, his evaluation of motivational factors will be colored by these preferences.[22]

In Strauss's case, his prior experience and intellectual inclinations led him to employ a medical, particularly a neurological, discourse for talking about childhood learning and behavioral problems:

> For the sake of clarity we wish to state that we shall follow in this discussion a neurological viewpoint, being aware that other interpretations are just as possible but that we consider this factor the outstanding one in understanding our methods of treatment and re-education of the brain-injured child.[23]

From this vantage point, Strauss and Lehtinen argued that the evidence that a child is brain-injured may be indirect. There may be no reliable proof that the child has experienced a birth trauma. There may be no neurological signs. In fact, there may be no indication save the kind of perceptual-motor and cognitive differences that Strauss and Werner identified in their comparative studies at the Training School. Taking their cues from the psychologist Arnold Gesell, Strauss and Lehtinen argued that we should not take for granted that children with learning and behavior problems were brain-injured. But they went on to say that we should recognize that any child can suffer a brain injury.[24]

As Strauss and Lehtinen saw it, the perceptual-motor and cognitive problems they identified in the children enrolled at the Training School were not only to be found among the mentally defective. They were to be found in children with cerebral palsy, in certain hearing impaired children, and most importantly in "children of normal intelligence with peculiar behavior."[25]

Four years later, in 1951, William Cruickshank of Syracuse University, who as a graduate student had worked at the Wayne County Training School, made an attempt to extend Strauss and Werner's work to a group of intellectually normal children. Working with his doctoral student, Jane Dolphin, Cruickshank replicated the perceptual-motor and concept formation tests that Strauss and Werner had used with a sample of intellectually normal children with cerebral palsy. They found that the test performance of these children, whose average I.Q. score was 93, was quite similar to the performance of the exogenous brain-injured children at the Training School, whose average I.Q. score was around 67.[26]

In 1955, Strauss again, this time in a volume co-authored with Newell Kephart of Purdue University, noted the need to expand the study of brain injury to include children with normal intelligence. Although they did not mention Cruickshank and Dolphin's study, Strauss and Kephart reported the existence of evidence to support the inclusion of normally intelligent children within the brain injury category:

> Recent surgical operations in adults have shown that considerable areas of brain tissue can be removed or rendered non-functioning without disturbing those functions which we measure with common administered intelligence tests. Clinical observations have revealed many cases of children in whom cerebral damage is present but whose intelligence quotients are at or above the normal levels. . . . We must therefore expand our concept of brain injury to include children with normal IQs.[27]

In support of their claim, Strauss and Kephart included in the volume's appendix case studies of thirteen children who were enrolled at the Cove School, an independent school for brain-injured children with campuses in Racine, Wisconsin, and Evanston, Illinois. The children featured in these case studies had normal intelligence but had been diagnosed as being brain-injured. They exhibited an array of school learning and behavior problems along with what Strauss and Kephart argued were indicators of brain injury, including paralysis, seizures, and abnormal electroencephalographs.[28]

V.

Strauss and Werner were neither alone nor were they the first, for that matter, to talk about low-achievement in neurological terms. I have already mentioned that a number of the early twentieth-century champions of backward children had speculated that childhood learning problems were the result of a central nervous system dysfunction. Between 1895 and 1917, James Hinshelwood, a Scottish ophthalmologist, published a number of reports concerning congenital word blindness, a severe disability in reading that appeared in individuals of normal intelligence as the result of damage to the area of the brain responsible for language.[29]

A decade before Strauss and Werner began their work at the Wayne County Training School, Samuel Orton, a neurologist at the Iowa State Psychopathic Hospital, undertook a series of studies funded by the Rockefeller Foundation that explored the neurological roots of language disorders.[30] As Orton saw it, language abilities were under the control of the individual's dominant cerebral hemisphere. For each individual, he went on to say, the dominant hemisphere was indicated by his or her laterality. In right-sided individuals—that is those whose right hand, right foot, and right eye are dominant—language abilities are governed by the left cerebral hemisphere. In left-sided individuals, the right cerebral hemisphere is responsible for the control of language. Adults who had suffered damage to their dominant hemisphere could exhibit an array of language difficulties including alexia or word blindness.[31]

Orton did not believe that word blindness was an apt description for this condition. He preferred the term strephosymbolia, which he defined as "twisted symbols." When individuals with this condition attempted to read, they routinely confused the orientation of letters and words. They mistook, for example, the letter *d* for *b* or the letter *q* for *p*. Similarly, they mistook a word such as *saw* for *was*.[32] During reading, according to Orton, individuals are in effect interpreting neural records of the stimuli, in this case letters and words, that are established in their dominant hemisphere. At the same time, their nondominant hemisphere is recording mirror opposites of these engrams.[33] If individuals suffer damage to their dominant hemisphere, they will attempt to decipher the engrams in their nondominant hemisphere, hence the reversals.

Orton noted that a similar condition could be found in

children who had not developed cerebral dominance. Because we only use one hemisphere for reading, children who failed to achieve cerebral dominance could easily attend to the reversed engrams in the nondominant hemisphere.[34] At the hands of Strauss, Werner, Orton, and no doubt many lesser lights, our way of talking about as well as our very understanding of childhood learning problems was reconstituted. What had once been an inexplicable condition with perhaps medical origins had become under their influence a full-fledged illness, brain injury.[35]

What Strauss, Werner, Orton, and others had done was to begin to medicalize the condition of childhood learning difficulties. Their research and resulting professional publications had the effect of first providing a medical label for a condition that had already been recognized as deviant behavior and then publicly announcing that label.[36] Parents, school managers, and the state itself would complete the process.

VI.

Medicalizing childhood learning difficulties would involve more than creating a new label for the condition. This new discourse would have to be used to mobilize efforts to obtain educational services for brain-injured children.[37] The impetus for these attempts were the parents of such children. In 1950 a group of Milwaukee parents concerned about the lack of understanding throughout the city of the school problems encountered by low-achieving, intellectually normal children established the Milwaukee Society for Brain-Injured Children. During the next ten years, the organization held seminars throughout the city to inform both parents and teachers of the existence of this condition.[38]

In 1958 another group of parents, this time in Richfield, Minnesota, a suburb of Minneapolis, were able to convince that city's board of education to establish a class for brain-injured children. Two years later, this same group of parents established the Minnesota Association for Brain-Injured Children. In addition, the organization was able to establish a weekend recreational club and a summer camp for these children, as well as a mothers club and a fathers-sons club.[39]

At about the same time, a group of parents in Birmingham, Alabama, frustrated by the absence of educational services for their children, organized the Alabama Foundation to Aid Aphasoid Children. Unable to convince the city's public school managers to establish a class for brain-injured children, the foundation hired its own teacher and established a private program supported by tuition payments, gifts, and the proceeds from a sale of pecans. In its first year, the foundation operated a single class with one teacher and three students. During the next three years, the foundation established two more classrooms, using the facilities of the University of Alabama and the city's schools. It secured the use of the city's child guidance and mental health clinics to evaluate children for brain injury, and began to place brain-injured children in the city's regular classrooms.[40]

Overall, these parental efforts bore mixed results. During the early 1960s, parent groups in Baltimore, New York City, and several cities in New Jersey were successful in securing the establishment of public school classes for their children. Other groups were less successful. Louisville's group, like their counterparts in Birmingham, had to establish their own private school. In Tulsa, Chattanooga, Memphis, and Lexington, Kentucky, parents secured some assistance from the public schools in the form of classroom space or the payment of teacher salaries. To obtain money for these ventures, these parent groups undertook a variety of fund-raising efforts and appealed to such philanthropic organizations as the Easter Seal Society, the Kiwanis Club, the Rotary Club, and the Junior League.[41]

An immediate problem facing these parent groups was the need to clarify precisely the difficulty their children were facing. In April 1963 the Fund for Perceptually Handicapped Children in Evanston, Illinois, sponsored a national conference in Chicago to explore the problems faced by brain-injured children and to consider how parental organizations could help such children. The highlight of the meeting was a keynote address by Samuel Kirk of the University of Illinois. Although Kirk's field of expertise was mental retardation, he had worked with brain-injured children, including spending several years on the staff of the Wayne County Training School.[42]

In his talk, Kirk told his audience about his dissatisfaction with the use of such terms as *brain injury* to describe the school learning problems of children who, as he put it, "do not have marked general intellectual deficits," but who "are unable to adjust in the home or to learn by ordinary methods in school." It made sense, Kirk argued, for researchers interested in identifying the biological roots of childhood behavioral deficits to use a term such as *brain injury*. What troubled him, however, was that the term offered no guidance to those who were responsible for educating these children. Kirk went on to tell his listeners that they should avoid "technical and complex labels" and instead "describe" the behavior of these children. He then introduced the term *learning disabilities* as representing what he believed to be the best behavioral description of the problems such children faced.[43] Kirk's remarks so swayed his audience that within a year the parent groups attending the conference joined together to form the Association for Children with Learning Disabilities.[44]

Although Kirk did provide a banner behind which parents of so-called brain-injured children could march, it was not clear how successful he was in clarifying the nature of this disability. Three years after his speech, a U.S. Public Health Service task force reported that there were at least thirty-eight terms that were then commonly being used by both professionals and lay persons to describe intellectually normal children with school learning problems. They included not only brain injury but such labels as *dyslexia, character impulse disorder, aphasoid syndrome*, and *hyperkinetic behavior syndrome*.[45] Whatever uncertainly already existed about the nature of this disability was only intensified by the existence of these multiple labels for referring to what was essentially the same problem.

VII.

Further exacerbating this difficulty were the conflicting explanations of learning disabilities being promoted by the field's early practitioners. During the 1960s there were as many explanations of learning disabilities as there were researchers working in this area. As we might expect, William Cruickshank, who had extended the ideas of Strauss and Werner to intellectually normal children, attributed this new disability to brain injury. Like Strauss and Werner, he argued that intellectually normal children could suffer a brain injury that would manifest itself in such behavioral deficits as hyperactivity, distractibility, and perseveration, characteristics that interfered with school learning. He went on to argue that such symptoms could also appear in children who were not usually thought of as having a brain injury. He noted that children with hyperactive emotional disturbance, for example, exhibited the same characteristics as brain-injured children and often responded to the same remedial strategies.[46]

Newell Kephart, who had worked at the Wayne County Training School and collaborated with Strauss in his research, saw learning disabilities as a mismatch between children's motor and perceptual abilities.[47] Kephart identified seven stages of childhood development. In the initial or motor stage, children learned to use their motor abilities to interact with their environment. They acquired information about the world through motor responses. In stage two, the motor-perceptual stage, children expanded their interaction with their environment by using their visual and auditory senses. At this stage it was necessary, Kephart argued, for children to be able to match the information that they received from their motor responses to that which they received through their senses. Both channels needed to provide them with the same information. In the following stage, the perceptual-motor, children discovered the greater efficiency of perception in exploring the world and consequently utilized their senses as the primary channel for obtaining information. Motor abilities became a secondary or back-up channel for obtaining information. Kephart then went on to describe the four remaining stages of development in which children were able to refine and integrate their perceptual abilities, thereby bringing greater efficiency to their learning.[48]

Key to the appearance of a learning disability, Kephart

argued, was the failure of the child at any stage of this sequence to develop a perceptual-motor match:

> Such a child lives, as it were, in two worlds: a perceptual world in which he sees, hears, tastes, smells, and the like, and a motor world in which he behaves and responds. In each of these worlds he has a mass, a body of information. Each body of information is at least relatively well structured. However, the two bodies of information are not matched. Therefore, he cannot use his perceptual activity to guide or influence behavior or response.

The result of such a mismatch, Kephart pointed out, was low-achievement. It could, for example, leave a child with the ability to identify letters or numbers, but be unable to reproduce them or to be able read, but not to write.[49] Like Cruickshank, Kephart attributed this condition to brain injury and emotional disturbance. But he also noted that the failure of children to develop key readiness skills as a result of the absence of critical learning experiences could result in learning disabilities.[50]

Samuel Kirk, however, was wary of attributing this condition to brain injury. Learning disabled children, he believed, were a diverse group. Some were clearly cognitively impaired. Many, however, had disorders in the psychological processes responsible for the reception, processing, and expression of language, problems that may or may not have been the result of brain injury. The emphasis placed on brain injury in explaining learning disabilities was, he thought, misplaced. It directed our attention at etiology when in reality our efforts should have been focused on remediation.[51]

The existence of these different and often conflicting explanations of learning disabilities made it difficult to establish the kind of widely shared understanding of this condition that would encourage the development of public school programs. In 1968 the National Advisory Committee on Handicapped Children, a committee authorized by the 1965 amendments to Title VI of the Elementary and Secondary Education Act to review U.S. Office of Education programs for the handicapped, sought to promote such an understanding with a definition of learning disabilities. According to the Committee, which was chaired by Kirk:

> Children with special learning disabilities exhibit a disorder in one or more of the basic psychological processes involved in understanding or in using spoken or written language. These may be manifested in disorders of listening, thinking, talking, reading, writing, spelling, or arithmetic. They may include conditions which have been referred to as perceptual handicaps, brain injury, minimal brain dysfunction, dyslexia, developmental aphasia, etc. They do not include learning problems which are due primarily to visual, hearing, or motor handicaps, to mental retardation, emotional disturbance, or to environmental disadvantage.[52]

As the product of a federal commission, this definition would come to have a certain official status. It would become the definition that the federal government and a majority of the states would use in their regulations concerning learning disabilities.[53] Yet it was a definition plagued with difficulties.

Writing in 1976, Patricia Myers and Donald Hammill identified four problems with the definition. First, they argue that there is little agreement among experts as to what are the so-called basic psychological processes. They believe that the term is so vague as to be virtually devoid of meaning. Second, they point out that to say "involved in understanding or in using spoken and written language" and then to say "which may be manifested in disorders of listening, thinking, talking, reading, writing, spelling, or arithmetic," is redundant. They claim that the two phrases mean precisely the same thing. Third, they believe that there is wide disagreement among experts about the meaning of such conditions as "perceptual handicaps" and "minimal brain dysfunction." To include them in the definition, Myers and Hammill argue, only adds confusion. Finally, they argue that it is virtually impossible to determine if learning disabilities are a primary or a secondary result of such conditions as mental retardation. They conclude their criticism by pointing out if the redundant and ambiguous elements were removed, the remaining definition would be so broad as to include all children with learning problems.[54]

Definitional problems were not, however, easily remedied. A 1969 report of the National Institute of Neurological Diseases and Stroke identified seven alternative definitions to the one offered by the National Advisory Committee. Learning disability, according to one of these definitions, could be a school learning problem resulting from a central nervous system dysfunction. It could also be a learning process problem having nothing to do with brain injury or even a school learning problem of unidentified origin.[55] Reviewing the status of research on what the report called the "central processing dysfunctions" of learning disabled children, the authors concluded that it would be difficult to establish any consensus about the nature of this condition:

> Because the characteristics exhibited by children with learning disabilities are diverse, there is no consistent behavioral pattern which identifies the group in question. This conflicts with the development of a definition which is descriptive of the group in question. Identification and definition are further complicated in that many of the behavioral symptoms found among children with learning disabilities are also found among normal or bright children who experience no difficulty in learning.[56]

Even if researchers could agree about the origins and causes of learning disabilities, they faced, according to the authors of this report, other difficulties. Whatever the dysfunction was, be it brain injury or something else, it was not readily observable without dissecting the brain. Researchers could undertake animal dissections and generalize their findings to humans, which needless to say was a risky venture. Or they could rely on autopsies of deceased humans. This latter procedure was also problematic. First, it was not clear where the researchers should look for brain damage. They were dealing with a minimal dysfunction that did not leave an easily recognized lesion, not gross brain damage. Second, it was not easy to locate deceased children. Most autopsy research was conducted with adults. And it was not certain that studies of adults could be extended to children.[57] These were difficulties that have, as we shall see in the epilogue, continued to plague learning disabilities researchers and practitioners.

VIII.

With the appearance on the scene of learning disabilities at the beginning of the 1960s, the movement to accommodate low-achieving children in the public schools underwent significant changes. First, there was, as I have already noted, a shift in discourse. What had been known at the beginning of the century as backwardness was now seen as a full-fledged neurological impairment. Second, the sponsors of this movement also changed. Early twentieth-century special classes were established at the behest of school managers as a means of enhancing their ability to administer an increasingly bureaucratic organization. The impetus for accommodating learning disabled children in the public schools came not only from educators but from the parents of these children.

What precisely mobilized these parents is, however, a bit unclear. Some contemporary researchers have argued that middle-class parents led the effort to establish public school programs for learning disabled children. To prove their claim, these scholars present a variety of evidence pointing to middle class leadership, most of it being indirect and suggestive. Much of their case rests on studies of enrollments in special education programs that show, they claim, that learning disabled classes are populated predominately by white, middle-class children.[58] The problem, however, is that there are at least as many if not more studies that point to the disproportionate representation of minority and lower-class students in these very same classes.[59]

There may be something to what these researchers are telling us about the role of the middle-class in championing the cause of learning disabled children. Most American reform movements, after all, are middle-class enterprises. But saying that does not really tell us much. On balance, their interpretation is not terribly compelling.

Another, and potentially richer, explanation attributes the emergence of learning disabilities to the post–World War II migration of Americans to the suburbs. An increasing marriage and birth rate during the early 1940s had created by mid-decade a demand for housing that the low housing starts of the Depression and the war years could not meet. In response to this housing shortage, a number of federal initiatives, including appropriations for mortgage insurance to support new construction and the establishment of mortgage loan programs for veterans, served to spur the construction of new single-family housing. Between 1944 and 1950, the construction of single-family homes increased from around one hundred thousand annually to about a million. The principal sites for this new construction were the suburban areas adjacent to the nation's major cities.[60]

According to this interpretation, living in the suburbs meant more to post–World War II families than affordable housing and pleasant surroundings. For young parents of the day, life in the suburbs symbolized the promise of opportunity and abundance. It would enable them to place their children at the center of their lives, thereby creating intimate and nurturing families. And it would be a setting that provided good and safe schools that would offer their children access to elite colleges and ultimately to good jobs and to an affluent lifestyle.

Suburban life, however, never lived up to these expectations. Families were never as intimate or nurturing as was claimed. A combination of factors, including financial worries, the frustration of women at the prospect of having primary responsibility for child rearing, and the absence of men from the home in response to the demands of work and commuting made for a family life that was often distant, cold, and tense. Similarly, suburban schools never delivered on their promise. The failure that had always affected large numbers of American children remained a salient feature of the supposedly good schools of the nation's suburbs. By explaining the school failure of their children as learning disabilities, suburban parents were able to rescue from imminent collapse the dreams that they held for their children and for which they had sacrificed their financial resources and emotional well-being.[61]

There are several reasons why invoking the concept of learning disabilities could offer suburban parents hope for their children. First, it provides a comforting explanation for their children's school failure. As noted in chapter one, attributing the cause of low-achievement to a neurological dysfunction means that children so afflicted are ill and thereby free from any responsibility for their problem. Similarly, looking at learning difficulties in this way removes any blame for the problem from either parents or schools. Second, it is an explanation of school failure that does not bear the stigma associated with backwardness and mental retardation. And third, educators routinely claim that special education can remedy the academic deficits associated with learning disabilities.[62]

Post–World War II suburbanization certainly could have created the social conditions that spawned the learning disabilities movement. Yet historians are only now just beginning to investigate this demographic transformation. We know that these suburban communities were diverse places. A few were affluent enclaves that could protect their inhabitants and their children from the vagaries of modern life. Most, however, were less wealthy, less exclusive, and ultimately less assuring places to be. Similarly, we know that very different kinds of people populated the suburbs. Some, no doubt, possessed the wealth, status, and security to provide their children with a life of abundance and opportunity. Most, however, were less successful and secure in their own lives and could offer their children a legacy that was problematic at best.[63] What we do not know, at least at present, is how appealing a learning disabilities explanation of low achievement was to such a diverse array of individuals living in such very different settings.

IX.

The campaign for educating learning disabled children during the 1960s, not unlike the effort to establish special classes for backward children earlier in the century, was directed toward contradictory purposes. In July 1969 the Education Subcommittee of the U.S. House of Representatives Committee on Education and Labor held hearings on the Children with Learning Disabilities Act. Introduced as an amendment to Title VI of the Elementary and Secondary Education Act, the legislation provided federal support for research on the causes and treatments of learning disabilities. The legislation would have the impact of completing the medicalization of learning disabilities by bestowing it with official recognition as a state designated handicapping condition.[64]

Much of the testimony indicated how establishing this special education category would help children with learning difficulties. W. Joseph Gartner, President of the Illinois Council for Children with Learning Disabilities, for example, noted the dilemma that parents of these children faced:

> We are the parents of children who, until recent years, had no official name for the kind of disability that handicapped them. Our children were relegated to the category of the mentally retarded or emotionally disturbed. Or, if they were not so severely handicapped, they were written off as lazy or branded as delinquent.[65]

Mrs. Leon Lock, President of the Pennsylvania Association of Children with Learning Disabilities testified about her frustrations in trying to obtain educational services for her son Andrew. Andrew, she noted, was a "bright" and "outgoing" child whose mental age was two years above his chronological age. Because he seemed to have difficulty when it came to "working with pencil and paper," Mrs. Lock had decided to wait until he was five and a half before enrolling him in kindergarten. Andrew's kindergarten experience was a disaster. He continually left his assigned seat and bothered the other students in his class. He was unable to do the work that he was assigned and was constantly reprimanded by his teacher. When given the first grade entrance test at the conclusion of kindergarten, Andrew received a score that was two years below his age level. Evidently attributing the problem to his behavior, school officials urged Andrew's parents to apply more consistent discipline.

What perplexed her about her son, Mrs. Lock stated, was that despite his learning and behavior problems, he appeared to have a strong desire to learn. Not knowing what to do, she and her husband sought to improve their parenting skills by consulting the county child guidance clinic. This effort proved unsuccessful. When the Locks noticed that Andrew did not constantly use one hand in picking up objects, they suspected that he might have a neurological problem. At first, they employed the training techniques that Samuel Orton had developed to treat children who had failed to develop cerebral dominance. When this effort showed no improvement, they took Andrew to a neurologist for an examination, including an electroencephalogram. The examination, however, did not reveal any neurological problems.

Mrs. Lock reported to the Subcommittee that Andrew spent two unsuccessful and disappointing years in public school until a school psychologist suggested that the child was brain-injured and belonged in a program for the mentally retarded. The Locks rejected this advice, removed Andrew from the public schools, and placed him in the Pathway School, a private school for learning disabled children. Mrs. Lock concluded her testimony by stating that so many of the difficulties that she encountered could have been prevented if there had been a greater recognition among school officials of the problem of learning disabilities.[66]

In his testimony to the Subcommittee, Representative Joshua Eilberg of Pennsylvania, a sponsor of the Children with Learning Disabilities Act, made clear to whom this legislation was directed:

> The programs which this bill would authorize are not designed only to serve children in the poverty areas of the Nation. The assistance which this bill will make possible will be available not on the basis of the average annual income in a given area but on where the problems are. I do not want to be misunderstood. I have supported programs which are designed to help our disadvantaged citizens. I have sponsored

legislation in their behalf and I will continue to do so. But I really do believe that too many of our educational programs have been overly directed to reaching the poor per se rather than reaching out to solve problems where they exist regardless of the economic condition of the person in the area affected.[67]

Much of the testimony presented to the subcommittee, however, addressed the threat that learning disabled children, if untreated, posed to the larger society. For the Subcommittee's Chairperson, Representative Roman Pucinski of Illinois, the existence of learning disabilities endangered social order. The nation, he warned, is:

> going to continue spending billions of dollars on public aid programs, on various programs dealing with social disorders, crime in the streets. We are going to see continued havoc and chaos if we don't address ourselves to problems of emotional instability in human behavior.[68]

A number of witnesses offered testimony that supported Pucinski's worst fears. Harold McGrady of Northwestern University noted that if the needs of learning disabled children were not met, they would "join the ranks of the maladjusted." He noted the view of a contemporary author that Lee Harvey Oswald may have been suffering from dyslexia.[69] In a letter to the Subcommittee supporting the legislation, Faires Kuykendall of Forth Worth, Texas, pointed out that approximately twenty percent of the nation's school children have learning disabilities and that the existence of this condition poses major societal problems:

> The problems of delinquency, crime and poverty are the consequence of ignoring the needs of these children, so normal and yet so handicapped. There is no doubt that there is a great savings in dollars and human values in attacking this problem at its source rather than paying for the consequences.[70]

Similarly Mrs. W.H. Wimberly of Lake Charles, Louisiana, pointed out in her letter to the Subcommittee that if a

learning disabled child did not obtain an appropriate education, he or she may become "a drop-out, a dope addict, a mur-
derer." And L.S. Holmes of Houston, Texas informed the Subcommittee that many learning disabled children end up as
school dropouts. He also noted that eighty-five percent of the
prison population of Texas were school dropouts. "I wonder,"
he asked, "what percent of these prisoners were brain-injured
with learning disabilities?"[71]

The message surrounding efforts to provide for learning
disabled children was, then, a conflicting one. For some, such
accommodations would help these children. Others, however,
saw this initiative as a means of protecting the nation from the
disruptive impact that the presence of the learning disabled
posed. Turn-of-the-century school managers, I argued in
chapter one, seemed caught between their desire to ensure the
educational progress of the most able students and their wish
to help disabled children. A half-century later, those supporting the education of learning disabled children faced a similar
quandary. They wanted to establish educational programs for
learning disabled children. They seemed divided, however,
about the purpose of these efforts.

X.

In this chapter, I have explored the transformation in our
understanding of childhood learning difficulties that occurred
between the mid-1930s and the end of the decade of the 1960s.
What was at the beginning of this period a somewhat diffuse
condition attributed largely to environmental but at times organic causes, was transformed, under the rubric of learning
disabilities, into a central nervous system dysfunction. We described this shift as an instance of the medicalization of deviance. This change in the way we talked and thought about
low-achievement occurred at the behest of different groups
with different goals. There were those psychologists, medical
doctors, and educators whose research on childhood learning
difficulties led to the appearance of a number of competing
organic explanations for this problem, an effort that culmin-

ated in the early 1960s in the creation of a concept of learning disabilities. There were the parents of low-achieving children who, comforted by an organic explanation of learning difficulties, organized to secure educational services for their children. And there were those public officials who saw those same educational services as a means of combating existing threats to social order. Taken together, their efforts inaugurated a movement to provide for children with learning difficulties not unlike the Progressive era effort to establish special classes.

In this vein I noted that initiatives to promote the education of learning disabled children appeared to reflect the same contradictory purposes that propelled forward the establishment of special classes. Both movements seemed undecided about whether their goal was to protect the abler segments of society or to help the disabled. How these contradictory purposes played out in actual school programs for learning disabled children remains to be seen. I will explore this topic in chapter five when we consider the development of programs for learning disabled children in the Minneapolis Public Schools. First, however, we need to pursue a subject that we introduced in chapter one and mentioned briefly in this chapter—namely, the role of private philanthropy in promoting accommodations for children with learning difficulties. It is this issue that we will examine in chapter four.

4

Private Philanthropy and the Education of Children with Learning Difficulties: From the Junior League School for Speech Correction to Whittaker Center

At its August 1966 meeting, the Atlanta Board of Education voted to establish a center for learning difficulties the following summer at its recently closed Whittaker Elementary School. As the Board of Education saw it, the city's greatest educational problem was that of the low-achieving child. These were children who were not really handicapped but whose difficulties in learning had attracted the attention of their teachers. As Superintendent John Letson noted, "there is great concern throughout the city for pupils of normal or higher intelligence who are physically sound but demonstrate inability to read." He went on to point out that the city currently offered classes for the emotionally disturbed and the mentally retarded. There was, however, at present, nothing being done for children who had difficulty in learning but did not fit into one of these acknowledged handicapping conditions.[1] The program that the Board approved would serve children in grades three to six who exhibited problems in reading, verbal communication, and visual-motor integration, difficulties that were just then beginning to be subsumed under the label of *learning disabilities*. Those selected would attend the Center full-time until the staff felt that they were able to succeed in a regular classroom.[2]

Not unlike Atlanta's first special and ungraded classes, Whittaker Center did enhance the capacity of the city's school managers to accommodate children with learning difficulties. Yet the Center was not solely a state initiative. Its establishment was the result of the efforts of the Atlanta Junior League, beginning with the opening in 1938 of its School for Speech Correction, to provide services for the city's speech and language impaired children. The events surrounding the establishment of both the Speech School and Whittaker Center point, then, to the role that private philanthropy has played, as I noted in chapter one, in initiating social welfare services, including provisions for disabled children. Ultimately the state, as also pointed out in chapter one, entered into such efforts. That involvement occurred only with the appearance of inadequacies in the League's administration of the Speech School. In this chapter, I shall examine the effort of the Junior League to establish its School for Speech Correction and explore how the city's school managers joined in this ostensibly private venture to create Atlanta's first public school program for learning disabled children.

Established in 1916, the Atlanta Junior League appeared on the scene fifteen years after Mary Harriman, daughter of railroad magnate Edward Henry Harriman, had established the Junior League for the Promotion of Settlements in New York City. And like its parent organization, the purpose of the Atlanta chapter was to provide a genial and sociable setting for debutantes while enlisting their efforts in the civic betterment movements of the day. As the *Atlanta Journal* reported in announcing the formation of the chapter, "though a social club, the higher objective and aim of the organization is charitable."[3]

The League was one player in a larger history of women's voluntarism. From the end of the eighteenth century onward, American women have created and affiliated with an array of voluntary organizations. Their reasons for doing so have varied. Some women directed their energies to any of a number of benevolent activities that sought to enlist their special talents and virtues in the moral redemption of the nation. Their efforts were directed at eradicating a host of social ills including slavery, drunkenness, prostitution, and impiety, to name but a few. Other women established study clubs devoted to promoting liberal culture and their own intellectual and spiritual transformation. And still others, under such rubrics as "municipal housekeeping," turned to the task of reforming the nation's political, social, and educational institutions. For some of these women, voluntarism would ultimately bring them into the political arena, first to secure the franchise and then to use their newly gained political power to transform society itself. Many, however, cared little about partisan politics and focused their energies on the work of benevolence.[4]

Although the League has from its inception played a major role in sponsoring and promoting a variety of charitable endeavors, its contributions have tended to be devalued, if not simply ignored. Writing in the June 1938 issue of *The Forum*, Struthers Burt made mention of the reform work of the League but then went on to accuse its members of self-indulgence and smugness in the face of the major problems of the nation and the world. He noted in this vein that at the same moment that the Philadelphia League was holding its annual bridge tournament, a report was issued that labeled that city's slums "the worst in the world."[5] The problem, as he saw it, was that:

> Junior Leaguers are so pleased with their social position and so quietly conscious of their good works that at any moment you expect roses to blossom in their handbags as they blossomed in the basket of Queen Elizabeth of Hungary while she was carrying bread across the snows to the poor.[6]

Ten years later, Cleveland Amory, writing in the *Saturday Evening Post*, noted a similar problem, which he attributed to the failure of the Junior League to live up to its purposes. The New York chapter of the League, he stated, had early in its existence established a day nursery to care for infants of the city's poor. "Somewhere, however, along in the shuffle from squash court to swimming pool to theater-ticket agency," according to Amory, "the ideal of taking care of the babies got lost." For many League members, he went on to say, the charitable events ceased to be a means of supporting social betterment, but had become ends in themselves.[7]

Notwithstanding these criticisms, Junior Leaguers were active in the work of benevolence. They focused their efforts on creating and sponsoring, both in conjunction with the state and as its surrogate, ameliorative institutions of one sort or another. In Atlanta it was a concern that made the education of speech and language impaired children a major focus of the Junior League's philanthropic agenda.

II.

While on a visit to New York City in the Fall of 1916, Isoline Campbell, a 1915 Atlanta debutante and daughter of the founder of Atlanta's Campbell Coal Company, heard about the League from a friend who herself was a member. Returning to Atlanta, Campbell held a meeting at the beginning of October for forty-five of the city's current and former debutantes at the exclusive Piedmont Driving Club to discuss the possibility of organizing a local chapter.[8] Securing widespread support from those in attendance, an application was submitted to the national office in New York and within a few weeks the Atlanta chapter was fully functioning. As its inaugural project, the members decided to hold a charity ball at the end of October at the Piedmont Driving Club. Known as the Butterfly Ball, the dinner-dance attracted four hundred Atlantans who paid two dollars and fifty cents each to attend. The event earned the League five hundred dollars which was donated to the Churches' Home for Girls. Part of the money was used to furnish a room in the Home for working women who earned no more than three dollars a week.[9]

Organized a year before the United States entered the war in Europe, many of the Atlanta League's first projects were war related. League members served both as volunteers in the canteen at Fort McPherson, an army base to the south of the city, and as hostesses to the troops stationed at the fort. In 1917 Campbell and five other League members went to France for a year as part of the Junior League Unit of the YMCA Canteen Service. As one of its early projects, the League established a Domestic Science Institute in downtown Atlanta that offered courses in cooking, sewing, and interior design in hopes of improving the efficiency of its participants in the "household arts." With the United States entry into the war, the Institute added courses in dietetics and canteen services for those members who had volunteered to help feed troops who were stationed in Atlanta.[10]

With the end of the war, League members were asked to volunteer for a host of citywide betterment efforts. In November 1919 members were urged to devote some time to working at a local convalescent home for children. And in February 1920 recruits were sought to prepare lunches for children attending Luckie Street School. During the following year, the Atlanta League also took responsibility through its Free School Library Committee to distribute books to underprivileged school children and through its Friendly Visiting Committee to send Christmas baskets to poor families throughout the city.[11]

Beyond volunteering for civic reform efforts, League members were offered opportunities to become informed about the important social and political events of the day, especially those affecting women and children. Between March and May 1921, the League with the help of Atlanta's Associated Charities offered a social service course, which included lectures on family living, community health, the care of disabled children, and education. Those completing the course received a social service certificate. And during the same period, the League's Legislative Committee presented a series of lectures for about thirty women at the Capital City Club on local government, children's legislation, the role of women's organizations, and women in industry.[12]

The following year, the chapter's Social Service Committee offered a course, entitled "What is Social Case Work." As part of the course, a group of eighteen members observed the work of visiting teachers at Grant Park School as they called on the parents of truant children. They then went on to assume the role of visiting teachers themselves and to investigate selected cases of truancy at the school.[13] To support these activities, the chapter continued its practice of hosting charity balls and inaugurated a number of new fund-raising activities, including the annual Junior League Follies, carnivals, golf matches, and a children's theater.[14]

Although members were urged to be aware of the important events of the day, the League was hesitant when it came to any direct political involvements. In her 1921 annual report, Atlanta Junior League President Anne Ryman commented on the decision of the chapter to establish a legislative committee to better inform the membership of state and federal actions affecting women and children. Taking pains to distinguish this action from the partisan political activities of other women's voluntary organizations, particularly those that had championed the cause of women's suffrage, Ryman noted that "we don't want to be tomahawk suffragists but we should not let ourselves be indifferent citizens." The purpose of the League, she went on to say, was "to make girls who have lived on the flesh pots of life realize their responsibility to those less fortunate."[15]

From its inception, Atlanta Junior Leaguers seemed especially interested in the problems of the disabled. In March 1921 one member suggested that the League host weekly tea dances and use the money they might raise to hold picnics for the city's disabled veterans. In October the League was asked to join with the Associated Charities, Rotary Club, Anti-Tuberculosis Association, and Overseas Club to help the Atlanta Board of Education to establish an open air school for anemic children. The League was to contribute $2700 annually for three years to furnish a surgical clinic and to pay the salary of a nurse and a dietitian. And later that month, Henrietta Davis of the Luckie Street School Committee reported that lunches would also be provided to children in the special class at Boulevard Street School.[16]

Throughout the 1920s the Atlanta League was seeking, as President Marion Sterns noted in her 1922 annual report, "some great work with which to identify ourselves." Sterns made the point that since the League was a women's organization, the project ought to be one that would aid women. She suggested the establishment of a permanent home for working women. That project, however, never materialized.[17] And the open air school was never begun. The contributions of the participating organizations arrived before the Board of Education was able to begin construction. Instead of rescheduling the project, the Board returned the money and decided that perhaps in the future they would establish the school using their own resources.[18]

The work undertaken by the Luckie Street School Committee did, on the other hand, prove successful. Reconstituted in 1922 as the Special Class Committee, it extended its work to provide lunches not only to the special class at Boulevard Street School but to the special classes at Luckie Street and Faith schools.[19] Those who participated in this project had especially high hopes for their efforts. Nellie Freeman, the Special Class Committee Chairperson in 1922, noted that their lunches were leading some students to improve their mental and physical conditions sufficiently to rejoin their regular classes. In her 1927 Special Class Committee report, Mrs. Clark Howell claimed that malnutrition was responsible for the placement of these children in special education.[20]

Despite their seeming success, the League's leadership was not satisfied with its programs. Reporting in 1928, the chapter president, Mrs. William Hughes, noted the organization's accomplishments but thought that it might be "scattering its labor and appropriations." The League could better use the resources that it had acquired through its growth during the 1920s, she thought, by supporting one major project. The members' choice was to raise $6,000 annually to support a charity ward at the city's Henrietta Egleston Hospital for Children.[21]

III.

Neither the school lunch nor book distribution program was continued beyond 1930. In its place the League concentrated its attention on supporting the Egleston charity ward and a thyroid clinic at Atlanta's Grady Hospital.[22] The League did, however, continue its work with the disabled. In 1936 the chapter became a sponsor of the Family Welfare Society's parent guidance project, an effort designed to help parents manage children with behavior and personality difficulties. The League contributed funds to pay the salary of a social worker to supplement the project's existing staff of a psychiatrist, psychologist, and medical advisor.[23] And two years later, the Atlanta League embarked on what would become its most ambitious philanthropic project, the establishment of its School for Speech Correction.

The impetus for the League's involvement with speech impairment was the arrival in Atlanta in 1936 of Katherine Cathcart Hamm. Child of a prominent Charleston, South Carolina, family and charter member of that city's Junior League, she received her early education in elite boarding schools, first Briar Cliff on the Hudson in New York and then the Burnham School in Northhampton, Massachusetts. Hamm's interest in speech impairment stemmed from her efforts to find a school that would teach her hearing impaired son from her first marriage to speak. Her search led her to St. Louis's Central Institute for the Deaf, where she enrolled her son in the school's oral program. While in St. Louis, she completed the Institute's four-year teacher training program and joined the school's faculty. After teaching at Central for two years, she moved with her new husband, William Hamm, a plastic surgeon whom she had met in St. Louis, first to Birmingham, Alabama, and then to Atlanta.[24]

Although her son was enrolled at a Connecticut boarding school by the time she had relocated to Atlanta, Hamm's interest in the education of the deaf continued. Upon arriving in the city, Hamm transferred her membership to the Atlanta League and joined Louise Davison, a speech teacher who conducted a private practice in her home, as a volunteer at the city's only free facility for speech correction, the Baby Clinic at Central Presbyterian Church. In May 1937 Hamm brought four young speech impaired children to a meeting of the Atlanta League to demonstrate the work being done at the Clinic. "Knowing the policy of the League to do pioneer work," Hamm later stated, "these children were shown to suggest a new project for the Atlanta League." With only Hamm and Davison working as part-time volunteers, it was not possible for the Clinic to serve all the city's deaf and speech impaired children, particularly those whose parents were too poor to pay for private therapy.[25]

Atlanta had established a special class for deaf children in 1912. That program, however, did not provide speech correction. In her 1938 report to the Board of Education, Belle McConnell, the city's lip-reading teacher, noted the difficulties that she had in meeting the needs of children for speech training. One of the problems was that both congenitally and noncongenitally deaf children were placed in her class. The congenitally deaf children did not typically possess oral language skills and instead used finger spelling to communicate. The non-congenitally deaf children, on the other hand, did have oral language skills that were, particularly if not used, in danger of deterioration. Parents of the non-congenitally deaf often complained about the practice of placing these two groups of children together in the same classroom. This setting, these parents argued, both offered poor models for hearing impaired children who could speak and limited their opportunity to use whatever language abilities they possessed. A second problem, McConnell reported, was that, according to a survey she had conducted, there were almost three hundred children in the city with "faulty articulation or definitely unintelligible speech," children for whom her class made absolutely no provision.[26]

The city's hearing impaired children could also attend the Georgia School for the Deaf at Cave Springs, some seventy miles north of Atlanta. Not unlike many other state schools, the Georgia School for the Deaf emphasized sign language and consequently did not offer speech training. Needless to say, Hamm, as an oralist, questioned the value of teaching sign language. It was, she admitted, easier for deaf children to acquire a manual mode of communication rather than to learn to speak. Once these children had learned sign language, she went on to say, they would be unwilling to exert the added effort needed to acquire speech. And lacking speech, they would be isolated from the mainstream of society. Hamm also noted that the state school would not accept children younger than seven, even though the best time to teach deaf children to speak was between the ages of three to six.[27]

At the League's May meeting, a committee was established to investigate how the group might assist the clinic. A month later at the Board of Directors' meeting, the committee recommended that the League contribute $1500 to pay the salary for a full-time teacher for one year. While looking for that teacher, the clinic moved to a larger facility when a local physician whose daughter was a League member offered to provide a vacant office in the city's Medical Arts Building at no charge until he could locate a paying tenant.[28]

Hamm believed that there were many Atlanta children with speech and hearing problems who were not being served by the clinic or the public schools. "These children seldom reach public schools, and their parents, from embarrassment or over-protection, would frequently hide their children from a stranger's inquiry."[29] What was needed, she felt, was a special school for these children. Otherwise, they will "become cases of charitable organizations for life whereas with the proper training, they can be rehabilitated and become wage earners and useful citizens."[30] At the February 1938 meeting of the League, a committee presented a three-year plan to develop a speech school with a full-time teacher. Three months later, members voted to actually create such a school and appointed Hamm to chair the Speech School Committee.[31] On June 6, 1938, the Junior League School for Speech Correction opened its doors with approximately fifty students and a single full-time teacher.[32] Initially, the Speech School offered these children individual therapy in twenty-minute sessions, two to three times a week. Over the next decade, the school would move three times to increasingly larger quarters, expand its staff to fourteen teachers, and serve over eight hundred adults and children in a variety of programs.[33]

One of the central concern's of the League from the beginning was to make the Speech School accessible to children who were not being served elsewhere. In a 1947 letter to Jeannie Wills of the Graham Oral School in Macon, Georgia, Rose Costello, the Speech School's Executive Director, reported that the school evaluated children without charge whether or not they were ultimately admitted, charged no entrance fee for admission, and used a sliding scale based on parental income to assess tuition. Parents who could afford to pay the full tuition were, she noted, asked to do so. Others were asked to pay what they could afford. And for the city's poorest families, tuition was assumed by the Department of Public Welfare.[34] As a consequence, the League had to provide increasing support for the school. In 1938, the year the school was established, the Junior League contributed $2,000 to its operation. Nine years later, the organization's direct contribution to the school had tripled to $6,500. In addition to its regular support for the Speech School, the League made additional contributions from the proceeds of its various social events.

In December 1939, for example, the League hosted what was to be its most publicized affair, a costume ball to celebrate the premier in Atlanta of the movie, "Gone with the Wind." The city auditorium, the site of the ball, was adorned with Confederate flags and pictures of Confederate heroes. The auditorium's stage was decorated to resemble the facade of an antebellum plantation. The ball's featured event was a grand march of guests dressed in Civil War era costumes led by Margaret Palmer, the Junior Leaguer selected as "Atlanta's Scarlett."[35] Among the invited entertainers was the all-black Ebenezer Baptist Church choir, which assembled in front of the plantation facade and sang a selection of spirituals. As the *Atlanta Constitution* saw it, it was a setting reminiscent of the old South:

> Magnolias, boxwood, and wisteria were present in profusion, giving great reality to the scene. Upon the portico walked a few folk in old fashioned costumes while the singing was in progress, as if it were a scene lifted intact from slavery times.[36]

The ball did, as it turned out, create some conflict in Atlanta's black community. At a meeting of the Atlanta Baptist Ministers Union the following week, Rev. G.W. Jordan criticized the Ebenezer choir for participating in the event. What bothered Jordan was that the city's blacks "were not granted the privilege of purchasing tickets" to an event commemorating a movie in which black actors played major roles. He further felt that the presence of the Ebenezer choir at the ball had conveyed the impression that Atlanta's black population voluntarily accepted the norms of racial segregation.[37] Excepting for this controversy, however, the ball was a triumph for the League and the city. The League garnered $20,000 from the event, of which half was contributed to the Speech School, the charity ward at Egleston, Grady's thyroid clinic, and numerous other philanthropic ventures.[38] Over five thousand people attended, including Clark Gable, Vivien Leigh, and other members of the cast, a host of Hollywood celebrities, the city's elite, and numerous politicians and other luminaries from throughout the nation.[39] According to the Atlanta Journal, the ball was a commemoration of the city's glorious past:

> Since Atlanta sprang up from a forest little more than a hundred years gone by, history has come to her in varying moods: sometimes sternly, always strikingly, but never so enchantingly as in the festival now begun. The past lives again in colors so warm and with a touch so intimate that it seems never to have died—or rather to have died and risen in new strength and beauty. The stars and bars flutter again along streets that echo far away the tramp of vanished armies.[40]

Despite the success of its money raising efforts, the League seemed concerned during the first decade of the school's existence about securing operating funds. The goal during this period was not only to secure sufficient revenue to run the school but to establish a $200,000 endowment. Throughout the 1940s, the organization's minutes make continual reference to the solicitation and receipt of contributions ranging from a gift of $100 by an Atlanta real estate agency to a $125,000 matching grant from an anonymous foundation.[41] A 1942 report of a visit to Atlanta by the Secretary of the Ways and Means Committee from the Junior League's national office in New York City, reported the desire of the Speech School staff to "obtain some paying patients."[42] The decision of the League to charge students tuition, albeit on a sliding scale, was made to allay this financial concern. Nonetheless, there was talk during these early years among the school's staff about the possibility of a private institution someday taking over operation of the Speech School.[43]

Despite its goal of being accessible, the Speech School did not provide services to Atlanta's black children. For a time in 1949, four Speech School teachers, all of whom were white, volunteered to provide speech instruction for black children at one of the city's black schools, Hill Street School. The League was not, however, happy with this arrangement. It wanted instead to find a way to provide a black speech therapist to serve the city's black children. The League had by this time established a cooperative teacher education program with Atlanta's Emory University, which did not admit black students. To resolve the difficulty, the League joined together with the Negro Women's Club and the University System of Georgia's Board of Regents to provide a scholarship to enable a black student to study speech pathology at Northwestern University in Chicago. Cecil Edwards, a graduate of Atlanta University, was awarded the scholarship and in 1951 began offering speech training in the city's black schools.[44]

IV.

The close association between speech and language impairments and other handicapping conditions, particularly those involving brain injury, led the Speech School from its inception to enroll a diverse lot of children. The first group of students attending the school included, as we would expect, children whose language problems were attributable to deafness, cleft palate, stuttering, and various articulation problems. There were, however, some children whose language impairments were of uncertain origin. One four-year-old child could understand what was said to him, but could not speak. Another child had learned to speak at eleven months, but could not presently speak after the onset of an unexplained paralysis. And still another child, as her mother put it, "doesn't seem to want to speak."[45] Despite this diversity in its student population, the Speech School was regularly urged to expand its services to accommodate an even greater variety of handicapped children and adults.

In 1945 Charles Strother, who directed the speech correction program at the University of Iowa, urged the Speech School to begin to conduct research on aphasia:

> There is also an urgent need for research on congenital aphasia. The Junior League Speech School would be in a position to do some important work in this field if a trained worker were available. Among the things that need to be studied are the effectiveness of different types of training programs, the nature of the learning process for these children, and the degree to which the condition responds to training. In a school such as yours where a number of cases are available and can be followed over a period of years, a good deal of important research might be done.[46]

Two years later, the Crippled Children League of Georgia approached the Speech School, the Atlanta Public Schools, and a number of social service agencies to develop a cooperative program for cerebral palsied and other physically disabled children.[47] And in 1954 the Junior League contributed almost $8,000 to the Speech School to pay the salary of a teacher of the multiply handicapped for a period of two years.[48] By the mid-1950s, the school included its original oral school for the deaf; clinics for individuals with cleft palates, cerebral palsy, and aphasia; a cooperative teacher education program with Emory University; a cooperative speech correction program with the Atlanta Public Schools; and day and evening programs for adults and children with speech and language impairments.[49]

Among the diverse groups of children who found their way to the Speech School were those with learning difficulties of inexplicable origin. They were children with problems not unlike those exhibited by students in Atlanta's first special and ungraded classes during the first two decades of this century, by the residents of the Cove School during the 1940s, and by those who would occupy the first public school classes for brain-injured children during the late 1950s and early 1960s. In June 1946 Ruth Davidson, a medical social worker at Grady Hospital, referred three children to the Speech School who had unexplained speech and language problems. Two of the children were sisters, Virginia, age nine, and Mattie, whose age was not given. According to their grandmother, both of these children were "slow in talking." Virginia was originally sent to Grady at age four "with the complaint that her vocabulary was limited and her stomach was too large." Mattie, according to the referral, "has speech difficulty, screams and holds her stomach as if it were aching when she is with Virginia." Davidson noted that she thought these children might be retarded, although she was not certain about that diagnosis.

The third child, Delano, age six, was referred to the Speech School because he had not made any attempt to talk until he was five and because he had problems in walking and hearing. Although his I.Q. measured 48 on the Stanford-Binet, the staff at Grady did not receive enough cooperation from Delano during the testing to reach any firm conclusions about his disability. They thought, however, that he actually possessed normal intelligence.[50]

Two months later, Robert Drane wrote the Speech School concerning his six-year-old son who had articulation problems, did not talk in complete sentences, and had poor concentration. As Drane put it, "we have a hard time keeping him at one thing for any length of time." The child had been attending a private school in Savannah, Georgia, operated by Eleanor Dudley for the previous two years. Because of the child's dislike for this school, it had been planned for him to enter the public schools during the coming year. Dudley, however, wanted to work with him for one more year. Uncertain about what was wrong with his child and what to do, Drane asked Hamm to arrange to have the child examined at the Speech School.[51]

What appears to have ultimately led the Speech School to create a specific program for children with learning difficulties was the staff's growing recognition about the actual heterogeneity of its student population. Until about 1951, the staff did little in the way of identifying the specific disabilities of the children who sought admission. Rather, they focused their attention on providing speech correction to whomever requested help. With the establishment of a diagnostic clinic in 1951, Speech School teachers became more attentive to identifying the specific disabilities of their students.[52]

One of their most perplexing difficulties in this regard was the presence at the school of children who exhibited learning problems that appeared to involve more than speech and hearing impairments.[53] Teachers did not often know precisely what was wrong with these children. In some instances, however, they reported these children as being perceptually impaired or brain-injured. As early as 1954, the school noted in its advertisements that it offered a program for brain-injured children.[54] In 1958 Tommie Parker, a speech therapist at the school, reported that there were about five children in her class for aphasics who did not really fit that diagnostic category. These children had normal intelligence, but they exhibited a variety of receptive and expressive language deficits. There were, Parker stated, other occasions thereafter where she encountered similar students.[55] A 1963 Speech School publication noted that the school currently operated three classes serving twenty-six children with "language disorders and perceptual distortions."[56]

The establishment at the Speech School of programs for children who were described as brain-injured or perceptually impaired during the 1950s and 1960s is not surprising. This was precisely the time, as we saw in chapter three, that the reconceptualization of low-achievement as a neurological problem was occurring nationally. If anything, the inclusion of children with learning problems of inexplicable origin among the Speech School's clientele lent credence to this discourse shift. Speech and hearing impairments were certainly problems of medical origin. It would not, then, be unreasonable to assume that the related learning difficulties that many Speech School students exhibited were also of medical origin. After all, what better group of professionals was available to legitimate a medical interpretation of childhood learning difficulties than were experts in the problems of speech and hearing impairment?[57]

V.

While Atlanta League members always seemed enthusiastic about supporting, both financially and with volunteers, the social betterment efforts of other agencies, they were less certain about whether they should be establishing anything as permanent as a school. Some of their reluctance was ideological in nature and reflected the goal of the Junior League to use its resources to initiate demonstration projects, which would ultimately be taken over by other agencies. In a 1951 speech to a Florida conference, Hamm noted that there were a number of agencies assisting the disabled. There was, however, always the need for one group to organize these diverse services, a task she described as that of "corralling resources."[58] Speaking to the Knoxville chapter of the Junior League five years later, Hamm pointed out that the task of educating the disabled belongs to "our educational systems, already geared for teaching, and to our welfare agencies." In establishing the Speech School, she went on to say, the League had initiated a service that the public schools and other state agencies seemed unable or unwilling to undertake. The League's work, as she saw it, was to operate the school for a time while garnering a cadre of supporters for speech correction work who would, at the proper moment, assume the task of "selling" responsibility for this service to the public.[59]

There were, in addition, practical considerations that made League members reluctant to enter into this project. During the 1930s, the Atlanta chapter was already lending its support to three major projects, Egleston's charity ward, the Grady thyroid clinic, and the parent guidance project. Littie Witherspoon, a field representative of the Welfare Department of the Junior League's central office, wondered if there was a real need for the Speech School in Atlanta. She thought that the Atlanta chapter might have to reduce its support to these other three projects if the group was to adequately support the Speech School.[60] Angelie Cox of Atlanta's Family Welfare Society noted that the establishment of the Speech School was creating a tense situation for the League. The organization, she noted, was "being pushed from several angles and they probably find it difficult to choose."[61] In a letter to Mary Lucas of the Child Welfare Association of America in March 1938, Virginia Howlett of the League's central office suggested that perhaps the Atlanta chapter should enter into its speech correction work as part of the parent guidance project.[62]

The establishment of the Speech School did, in fact, cause the League to rethink its commitments. In November 1940, Helen Lipscomb of the Junior League's Community Service Department suggested that because of the merger of the Grady thyroid clinic into another unit of the hospital, it was time for the Atlanta chapter to withdraw its support. That same month, Lipscomb noted the increasing tension in some of the Egleston Hospital staff who saw themselves in competition with the Speech School for the same limited financial resources.[63] Florence Van Sickler of the Child Welfare Association of Fulton and Dekalb Counties suggested that the League should invite Atlanta's Superintendent of Schools, Willis Sutton, to join a proposed Speech School Advisory Board as a means of setting the stage for transferring control of the school to the Board of Education.[64]

Contributing to the uncertainty of League members about the Speech School was Hamm's role as Director. In a 1940 visit to Atlanta, Helen Lipscomb noted that Hamm was regarded as "a sort of heroine" by the Speech School's Board of Directors. She single-handedly assumed responsibility for virtually all the school's day-to-day operations. Yet, according to Lipscomb, Hamm lacked the administrative skills needed to ensure the school's efficient operation. Volunteers, for example, were often unsupervised and not clearly told of their responsibilities. Hamm's administrative style appeared to hamper fund-raising. The Speech School had an Advisory Board whose members were appointed because of their influence with community organizations, which might, in turn, make financial contributions to the school. Hamm, however, never relied on this Board for securing funds. Rather, she raised funds by having Speech School children offer public demonstrations of their accomplishments during which time she solicited money from those in attendance. Similarly, she did not involve the Advisory Board in formulating policy for the Speech School.

A particular problem that the school faced during its first decade of operation, Lipscomb noted, was Hamm's failure to develop an admissions policy. Hamm simply allowed those children who she felt belonged in the school to attend. At one point it turned out that Hamm was personally admitting children from outside the city when there was a waiting list of about two hundred Atlanta children who wished to attend the school. Hamm, it seems, had a great distrust of psychiatrists and social workers. She did not use psychological tests in evaluating children who applied to the school. Hamm, in Lipscomb's words, "stated that she knew more about whether a child was mentally average than anyone else and that the use of social welfare agencies for helping her understand the social background was a waste of time."

It was difficult, according to Lipscomb, to get Hamm to admit to her administrative weaknesses. The Speech School's Board of Directors tried to improve the situation by lessening Hamm's apparent burdens in running the school. At one Board meeting it was decided to involve more volunteers in the school's operations, to obtain needed statistical information about the student body, and to shift responsibility for managing finances from Hamm to a volunteer. Yet making these changes was difficult. During the meeting, according to Lipscomb, "Mrs. Hamm became highly emotional and wept, so nothing was discussed, excepting by mutual agreement with her." Hamm, again in Lipscomb's words, said that "she was unable to give the Board advice as to what was needed in personnel."[65] As Florence Van Sickler pointed out in a 1942 letter, Hamm was "very possessive" when it came to the Speech School. "She was," Van Sickler went on to say, "emotionally tied up in it, I think, because of her own child who had a speech difficulty."[66]

Taken together, the League's preference for short-term demonstration projects, its competing financial commitments, and Hamm's administrative failings represented significant obstacles to the smooth operation of the Speech School. Despite its leadership in providing services for Atlanta's speech and language impaired children, there were indications that the League may not have had the capacity to sustain this initiative on anything approaching a permanent basis.

VI.

Atlanta's public officials were aware of the League's difficulties with the Speech School and responded with financial support. In 1944 the Fulton County Welfare Board contributed $5,000 to the Speech School, and the Atlanta Board of Education offered to pay the salary of one speech teacher at the school.[67] Despite these grants, there was no legal mandate in Georgia that required the public schools to educate handicapped children, nor was there any financial support for local school systems that voluntarily established their own special education programs.[68] The following year, however, the League began to initiate efforts to secure this financial assistance.

Hamm approached State Senator Sam J. Welsch of Cobb County, who knew one of the children attending the Speech School, to ask him to support an enabling act that would allow local school systems to establish special classes for deaf and speech impaired children, and would provide state aid to pay the salaries of teachers assigned to these classes. Welsch was able to secure the help of Governor Ellis Arnall, whose grandfather had been a trustee of the Georgia School for the Deaf and who had several deaf relatives. With Arnall's support and with the lobbying efforts of the League, the bill was enacted.[69] As a result of this legislation, the Atlanta Board of Education agreed to pay the salary of a second teacher at the school. And in 1947 the Board agreed to pay the salary of a third teacher, who instead of being placed at the Speech School would carry out her duties in the city's public schools.[70] By 1948 over half of the Speech School's budget came from public school contributions, while only about thirteen percent came from the League.[71] And four years later, the Atlanta Board of Education was paying the salary of eight speech school teachers who worked on an itinerant basis in the city's schools.[72]

Junior League members, as it turns out, disagreed about how the Speech School should respond to the introduction of state aid. Some believed, as I have already stated, that the League should support only demonstration projects and advocated turning the Speech School over to the public schools at some future date. They believed that the cooperative arrangement between the League and the Atlanta Public Schools represented a good start, but that eventually the city would require a single agency that would address all phases of special education.[73] As Speech School President Mary McCarty noted in a 1953 letter, the task of the League was to "lead along our whole lagging State into an acceptance of special education—the common schools, our higher education institutions, our government agencies of health and welfare."[74]

Others, however, were worried about the advisability of turning the Speech School over to state authority. It would, they felt, be less costly to provide special education through a single institution, such as the Speech School, rather than to offer these services in each of the city's schools. They also believed that placing the Speech School under the control of a public agency would subject it to the "vagaries of politics." Hamm was particularly outspoken about transferring the responsibility of the Speech School to the Atlanta Board of Education. "Do not locate where your control might be jeopardized. An interested superintendent may be friendly toward speech programs but when he goes out of office, there is a chance that his successor may not be sympathetic with the idea."[75]

There was, however, little impetus for the Board of Education to assume responsibility for the Speech School. Georgia's 1949 school funding legislation did not provide any additional money to support public school special education programs beyond that which was provided in the 1945 enabling act.[76] In 1950 the Board of Education in Moultrie, Georgia, was able to obtain $2100 through the enabling act to support the salary of one speech correction teacher. Atlanta, despite the fact that the League had supported this legislation, was unable to obtain any state funds to pay its speech teachers. The problem was that this legislation provided state aid for public schools, not private agencies. Moultrie's speech teacher was a city employee, while Atlanta's speech teachers worked for the Junior League.[77]

Within a decade the situation would change. One of the largest contributors to the Speech School during this period was the Atlanta Board of Education. Between 1957 and 1961, the Board provided anywhere between $18,000 and $20,000 a year for educating children enrolled at the Speech School. The availability, however, of Board-supported Speech School teachers in the public schools served to decrease Speech School enrollments, which, in turn, increased the per-pupil cost for the children remaining at the school. During the 1957–1958 academic year, the Board supported twenty-six students at the school at a cost of $760 per child. Three years later, the Board was supporting eighteen children at the Speech School at a cost of $1222 per child.

These expenditures, along with similar support for orthopedically impaired children enrolled at the Cerebral Palsy School and at Aidmore Hospital, represented costs to the Board that were not reimbursable by the state. Reporting to the Board of Education at its October 1961 meeting, Superintendent John Letson noted that it would be cheaper if the city operated its own speech correction program. He noted that if the Board hired a teacher at the average salary that year— $4,942—and assigned that teacher to a class of five children, the minimum that the state required for speech correction classes, the cost for each child would be $706. The city would save $416 for each child over what it was costing the Board to place that child at the Speech School.[78] Three years later, the state would increase the incentive for Atlanta and other local school systems to establish their own special education programs for all handicapped children by authorizing the use of state funds to support the cost of such efforts.[79] It was in fact the availability of these funds that led Atlanta to establish Whittaker Center.

A major problem facing Atlanta in establishing the Center was securing the projected first-year operating costs of almost $70,000. State funds would cover some but not all of these costs. The Board was able to use approximately $16,000 from its two million dollar ESEA Title I grant to cover the cost of children who had already been diagnosed as having learning problems. To secure additional funds, the Board turned to the Junior League which voted to contribute $25,000 to the Center during its first year.[80] The League would continue to provide financial support for Whittaker Center for the next five years, in addition to providing volunteers to work with individual children and to relieve teachers who were busy recruiting students.[81] In 1968, a year after Whittaker Center opened, the question of Atlanta's responsibility for providing special education became academic. That year, the Georgia General Assembly passed legislation requiring local schools within a period of two years to establish and support, with the help of state funds, their own special education programs.[82]

VII.

In Atlanta it took the interplay between the public schools and the Junior League to provide services for children with learning difficulties. That same interplay, however, had the ultimate effect of institutionalizing barriers to common schooling. In 1960 the Speech School, recognizing its increasing dependence on public school financial support, severed its ties with the Junior League and became a nonprofit, independent institution. Such a change, its supporters believed, would place the institution in a stronger position to solicit the increasing financial assistance its operations now required.[83]

The League, on the other hand, went on to other ventures, including the support of a public school program at Whittaker Center. By the end of the decade of the 1960s, Atlanta had two programs, one private and the other public, for learning disabled children. What began, then, as an effort to address the inaccessibility of the city's schools to children with speech and language impairments resulted in the creation of new public services for them. At the same time, however, the very same initiative brought into existence on a more permanent basis an alternative, private system for accommodating these same children.

Writing about another phase of welfare provision, the

creation of employee benefit programs, the sociologist Beth Stevens notes the impact of this division between public and private provisions:

> In one sense, public and private programs have served as pressure valves for each other. The establishment of a welfare program by one sector has reduced the pressure on the other sector to satisfy certain needs. The establishment of Social Security relieved private corporations of the responsibility for maintaining pensions for poorly paid workers, and the development of private health insurance reduced the pressure for national health insurance.

As Stevens sees it, private programs typically serve small, often the more privileged, segments of the community, while public programs serve those who remain.[84] This is precisely what occurred in Atlanta. The Speech School ceased to be an adjunct of the city's public schools and became instead its competitor and a refuge for those who sought to escape them. It was the first of what are today seven exclusive, independent day schools throughout the city and adjacent suburbs that serve for the most part the learning disabled children of the wealthy. Whittaker Center eventually evolved into an array of services in the city's public school classrooms to accommodate the low-achieving children of the less affluent.

VIII.

Exploring as we have in this chapter the work of the Atlanta Junior League in establishing the Speech School and in supporting Whittaker Center tells us much about the joint role which the state and private philanthropy have played in creating social welfare services. Philanthropic groups such as the League often took the initiative to provide these services. State involvement, in the form of financial support or direct control, occurred only later in response to the inadequate operation of the services on the part of private philanthropy.

Atlanta's school managers, we saw in chapter two, had during the early years of this century established special and ungraded classes to accommodate some children with learning difficulties. They did not, however, provide any services for speech and language impaired children. That task, which led ultimately to the establishment of programs for the learning disabled, fell to the Junior League. In this chapter we saw how a combination of factors, including the Junior League's philanthropic strategy, its existing involvements, and Catherine Hamm's leadership, signaled problems in the League's administration of the Speech School. The response to these difficulties on the part of Atlanta's school managers was first to provide financial support to maintain this private venture and ultimately to create its own services in the public schools. The Speech School did not simply disappear from the scene. Reorganized as an independent day school, it took on a new role as an alternative to the services provided by the city's public schools. As a consequence, this attempt to make the schools more accessible to Atlanta's low-achieving children served in the end to undermine the principle of common schooling.[85]

The establishment of the Speech School points, albeit in a different way than we have previously considered, to the contradictory purposes surrounding the attempts of school managers to accommodate students with learning difficulties. In establishing special classes, Progressive era school managers seemed unable to decide if their goal was a system of public schooling that served all children or just the most able. The sponsors of the Speech School seemed equally unsure. Were they creating an institution that would have the effect of rendering the public schools more accessible to all children? Or were they establishing one that would serve only some children, perhaps the more affluent, while consigning the rest to the public schools? It did not turn out to be a dilemma that they could resolve.

Private philanthropy, we should however note, was not always the initiator of services for children with learning difficulties. In Minneapolis, as we shall see in the next chapter, it was the city's school managers who took the lead in making provisions for these children. As a consequence, the interplay between the state and private philanthropy would be different than it had been in Atlanta.

5

The Struggle for School Reform in Minneapolis:
Building Public School Programs for
Low-Achieving Youth, 1930–1970

The presence of low-achieving children in the public
schools, as it turned out, posed a rather knotty problem for
school managers ostensibly committed to a common school
ideal. They could not simply establish special classes and be
done with it. The effort of Atlanta's school managers to develop
the administrative capacity to accommodate children with
learning difficulties led them to a long term and complicated
relationship with private philanthropy that in the end seemed
to confuse rather than to resolve the problem.

In this chapter, I will explore the intricacies that this kind
of state-building entailed in the public schools of Minneapolis,
Minnesota, during the years between 1930 and 1970. It was
during this period that Minneapolis school managers introduced a succession of bureaucratic reforms that they hoped
would accommodate children with learning difficulties. Not
unlike their counterparts in Atlanta, they sought to reconcile
their desire to protect regular classroom teachers and students
from the supposed disruptive influence of low-achieving children with their goal of being accessible to all children. In the
end, as we shall see, they were no more successful than their
Atlanta colleagues in resolving the seemingly contradictory
purposes to which they were directing the city's schools. And,

just as in Atlanta, the attempt of private philanthropy to resolve matters complicated them further.

II.

At the turn of the century, Minneapolis was Minnesota's
largest city with a population of just over two hundred thousand. Incorporated as a village fifty years earlier, Minneapolis
had during the last half of the nineteenth century become a
railroad hub for the upper Midwest, an employment mecca for
migrants from adjacent rural areas and for European immi-
grants, and an important site for the nation's flour and lumber
milling industries.[1] During the next thirty years, increasing
migration to Minneapolis coupled with the growth of the city's
commercial and service sectors virtually doubled the population to over four hundred thousand.[2]

Although Minneapolis's first public schools predate its in-
corporation by several years, a citywide school system was not
established until 1878, six years after Minneapolis and the
adjacent village of St. Anthony were consolidated into a single
municipality. Initially enrolling some five thousand students,
the next half-century witnessed significant growth. In 1900 the
city schools enrolled about thirty-six thousand students in four
high schools and sixty grammar schools. By the late 1920s,
Minneapolis enrolled eighty-five thousand children in eight
high schools, eight junior high schools, two vocational schools,
and ninety elementary schools.[3] Not unlike the situation in
Atlanta and in other cities, turn-of-the-century school managers in Minneapolis saw special classes as providing them with
expanded administrative capacity to deal with low-achieving
students. In 1900 the city established its first ungraded school
to provide "for those pupils who do not comply with the rule of
the public schools concerning attendance and conduct."[4] In
1910 the Board of Education established a program for stam-
merers and two years later opened a class for mentally retarded children. In 1915 the Minnesota Legislature passed a
bill that permitted the state's school districts to establish special schools and classes for instructing deaf, blind, speech im-

paired, and mentally retarded children. It provided these districts with a $100 stipend for each handicapped child enrolled in any of these special programs. With the passage of this legislation, Minneapolis began to expand its special education services. By 1925 the city was providing special programs for children who were blind, orthopedically handicapped, deaf, speech impaired, anemic, and mentally retarded.[5]

The development of special education fitted well with the concern over low-achievement that preoccupied the attention of Minneapolis's school managers during the 1920s. In his 1924 annual report to the Board of Education, Superintendent William F. Webster noted a failure rate of "seven to nine out of one hundred pupils" in the elementary schools and "seven to nine out of one hundred subjects taken" in the high schools. Failing students, he went on to say, were costing the city $500,000 a year. It was, as he put it, "no inconsiderable trifle."[6] In his subsequent reports throughout the decade, Webster continued to note the additional costs which the city had to bear as a consequence of this recurrent failure.[7] As Webster saw it, there were a number of solutions. School managers had to ensure that the curriculum allowed children to make reasonable progress. Likewise, they had to ensure that competent teachers were available throughout the city. Finally, parents of failing children, he argued, had a responsibility. They needed to overcome their fears and admit that their children were having difficulties. And they needed to be willing to place them in special education.[8]

Student failure continued to concern the city school managers during the decade of the 1930s.[9] Yet the Depression brought a related issue to center stage—namely, the increasing enrollment of low-achieving children. Although annual enrollment increases during the decade of the 1930s were lower than those of the previous decade, total enrollment during the Depression increased. In 1928 Minneapolis enrolled eighty-five thousand children. Four years later, in 1932, about ninty thousand children attended the city schools. Of particular concern to school managers was the distribution of this increase. Elementary enrollments were decreasing while those at the high school level were increasing. During the period from 1923 to 1934, for example, the number of children under sixteen attending Minneapolis schools decreased 9.7 percent and the number over sixteen increased 71.8 percent. At the root of this problem was the decline in employment opportunities for high school graduates. Between 1929 and 1932, the unemployment rate for high school graduates increased from 8.4 percent to 30.9 percent. As a consequence, a large number of low-achieving children who would have under other circumstances left school for work, now remained in school.[10]

The Depression forced Minneapolis school managers to provide for this increasing number of students with decreasing revenues. In 1931 the city's Board of Estimate and Taxation ordered a ten percent decrease in the school budget. The following year, school expenditures were reduced another ten percent. In 1933 another budget reduction took place, this time amounting to seventeen percent. Total revenues were cut from over eight million in 1931 to six million in 1933.[11] Nevertheless, the city instituted a number of curriculum reforms to accommodate what was becoming a less able school population. Some of the innovations sought to preserve a common curriculum for all students by introducing some minor modifications to create a more functional and hopefully more attractive course of study for children with academic difficulties.[12] Other initiatives involved the establishment of segregated, special programs of various sorts to provide for children with learning difficulties.

Reporting to the Minneapolis Board of Education in September 1933, Adner Heggerston, a school system research assistant, noted the conflicting goals that led the city to establish its first special education programs. He pointed out that one of the hallmarks of American society was the access it offered each child to equal educational opportunity. Such access did not require, he pointed out, that all children be provided with the same educational experiences. Some children exhibited learning and behavior problems that interfered with their progress in regular classrooms.[13] These children needed to be educated in special settings:

> Segregation has been practiced on the theory that it benefited the handicapped child and also the members of the class from

which he was removed. By relieving the teacher of a difficult problem, it would allow her more time for the normal pupils, with consequent benefit to them. This form of relief was all the more welcome to the teacher since the atypical children, especially those with a mental handicap, usually furnished more than their share of behavior problems.[14]

Mentally retarded children, according to Heggerston, were more likely than other children to engage in truancy, tardiness, lying, temper tantrums, abusive behavior, and obscenities.[15]

In addressing the problems posed by these children, Heggerston noted, many Minneapolis educators were unaware of the great degree of heterogeneity within this student population. It was common practice in the city at that time to place all children with I.Q.s between 50 and 80 in the same special class. He recommended instead that the higher functioning children "be associated with other dull normals with I.Q.'s above 80 rather than with feeble-minded children." He urged the city to find a way to accommodate these children while avoiding the creation of more special classes.[16]

III.

Beginning in the 1930's, Minneapolis began experimenting with alternatives to the special class for educating these backward or slow-learning students. Writing in March 1932 to the principal of Bryant Junior High School, Assistant Superintendent Prudence Cutright suggested two such schemes. A series of modified courses could be used that were designed for children with learning problems. Although these courses would bear the same title as regular junior high school offerings, they would be more applied and related to the day-to-day concerns of young adolescents. Social studies, for example, would be redesigned so that it would include content on community civics, and mathematics would be modified so that it would emphasize basic arithmetic skills. A second scheme would place slow-learning junior high school students in regular classes for the first semester, during which time counselors would undertake an evaluation of each of these children. Based on the results of this study, an appropriate program would be designed for each of them for the second semester.[17]

A year later, Barbara Wright, the Supervisor of Counseling, in a letter to a New Orleans school board member identified several experiments that were then being undertaken in Minneapolis to assist junior high school students who were having difficulty in their regular classes. At Jordon Junior High School, all seventh- and eighth-grade students were being passed on to the ninth-grade. Those who began exhibiting difficulties in the ninth-grade were placed in a special group that was allowed to remain in this grade for three semesters instead of the usual two. At Lincoln Junior High School, seventh- and eighth-grade students who were having difficulties were assigned for a half-day to a special teacher who provided instruction in the academic subjects while remaining in their regular classes for homeroom, art, industrial arts, and physical education. And at Phillips Junior High School, the counselor conducted case studies of the entering children. Those identified as being below average were placed in low-ability groups that offered a modified curriculum. These experiments, Wright noted, were not designed to permanently separate low-ability children from their more able peers. Such a separation should, she argued, be avoided. It would implicitly teach less able children that they were inferior to children of higher ability. And once having been separated, these less able children would have difficulty learning how to interact with children of different abilities. Similarly, she suggested that it was undesirable to segregate low-ability children in special schools.

Wright also noted that vocational education was not the necessary answer to the problem of the low-achieving child.[18] At about the same time, high school teachers were also developing modified courses for low-ability children. In May 1933, for example, John Greer, Principal of West High School, reported that his teachers had developed modified courses in tenth-grade English, social studies, and mathematics.[19]

Elementary teachers were also faced with the necessity of

accommodating slow-learners.[20] The results of a 1935 survey of the city's first-grade teachers revealed, however, that they disagreed about what should be done with these children. Most of the seventy teachers surveyed indicated that they identified slow-learners from information about their children's mental ability, experience, vision and hearing, language ability, and interest in school. Seventeen teachers, however, stated that they did not consider the question of children's experience in identifying slow-learners. Twenty-four teachers indicated that they paid no attention in their evaluations to children's visual and hearing abilities. These teachers were also divided as to the kind of organizational modifications they introduced into their classes to teach slow-learners and the time at which they introduced systematic reading instruction to these children.[21]

The city's teachers, as it turned out, disagreed among themselves about the wisdom of creating a differentiated program for slow-learners. Early in 1938, Assistant Superintendent Cutright appointed the Sub-Committee on the Slow-Learning Pupil, composed of teachers throughout the city, to advise the administration about needed curriculum changes.[22]

In May of the same year, Cutright issued a report indicating that the Sub-Committee might be working at cross purposes from the General Curriculum Committee, a group of teachers who were currently undertaking a study of the entire school program. The Sub-Committee, for example, recommended that slow-learning children required not only instruction in the basic skills but the opportunity to participate in enrichment activities. The General Curriculum Committee, however, pointed out that slow-learning students "become confused" when offered too many options. The Sub-Committee recommended that reading material be purchased that took into account the fact that the mental age of slow-learning students was often lower than their chronological age. The General Curriculum Committee felt that it was difficult to determine what mental age is required to read a particular book: "A child who is interested in a book will overcome great obstacles in reading it, whereas another child of an even higher mental age who is not interested in the book will not exert himself to understand it."

Finally, the Sub-Committee recommended that classes for slow-learners be limited to twenty-five children. The General Curriculum Committee felt that class size should be reduced for all students and that it was not clear that this reduction should be offered for slow-learners when above-average students were also suffering when placed in large classes.[23]

The most frequently voiced recommendation during the 1930s for addressing the problem of low-achievers was that of reducing class size. In 1937, Katherine Masley, a teacher at Pratt Elementary School, reported on her efforts with so-called backward children, some of whom were, as she put it, "anti-social in attitudes." Masley identified a group of seventeen fifth-graders in her combined fifth- and sixth-grade class who were not making adequate progress. These children were "very slow in finishing their work, quiet, ready and willing to follow, satisfied to let others make contributions to discussions." Two of these children, she noted, had exhibited inappropriate behavior on the playground. Masley was interested in determining what would occur if these seventeen children were placed in a class by themselves.

When placed in this smaller class, she noted that these children began to improve. They seemed, among other things, to be more interested in class activities, to be more aware of the errors they made in completing assignments, and overall to understand better what was required of them. In her report, Masley stated that the achievement test scores of these children increased during the course of the year. At the beginning of the experiment in September, the mean test scores of these children were fifty-two percent in arithmetic fundamentals, twenty-four percent in arithmetic problem solving, and forty-eight percent in reading. In June, the mean scores were eighty-two percent in arithmetic fundamentals, thirty-one percent in arithmetic problem solving, and sixty-two percent in reading.

For Masley, these gains in achievement were not the most important result of this experiment. What impressed her more was the improvement in the social behavior of these children.[24] During the next decade, the small class would in fact become the mainstay of the state-building efforts of Minneapolis school managers as they sought to deal with the problem of low-achievement.

IV.

In 1943, Minneapolis introduced a system of annual promotions to replace its existing practice of promoting students at the conclusion of each semester. As a consequence of this new policy, children in the secondary grades who failed a subject would now have to repeat an entire year's work in that subject, not, as had been the case, a semester. Fearing that this change would increase failures among his less able students, Newton Hegel, Principal of Folwell Junior High School, devised a solution that came to be known as the Small Class or B Curriculum Experiment. With the assistance of the school's counselor, Eva Bergeland, he set about to identify those seventh-graders who he thought were most likely to experience academic difficulties. These students were then assigned to English, social studies, and mathematics classes with enrollments of about twenty, which was half the size of the typical class at Folwell.[25]

Initial reports indicated that placing these students in smaller classes had a positive effect, at least on the attitudes of these children. Writing in the Spring of 1945, Folwell seventh-grader Diane Crew praised the small size of her class. "You have more time to think about things. You feel more freely about talking and asking questions. In a big class you seem to get behind all the time." She went on to describe how this class had benefitted her: "It helped me in understanding more things and thinking more clearly with out [sic] stumbling along. It also helped me in reading much better and spelling better."[26]

In a May 1945 letter to Superintendent William Goslin, Hegel noted that he had originally thought that teachers would have to modify the curriculum to reduce the failure rate among these low-achieving students. In fact, however, he found that extreme modifications were not necessary. The reduced size enabled teachers to provide students with sufficient individual help to improve not only their academic performance but their attitudes toward school. Some of these students, Hegel pointed out, improved sufficiently and were able to return to their regular classes. In order to allow those students who needed to remain longer in the Small Classes to do so, Hegel had that year used existing faculty to expand the program to the eighth-grade. His letter to Goslin requested the assignment of an additional teacher to Folwell the following year to enable him to extend the program to the ninth-grade. To justify his request, Hegel offered to provide the Superintendent with information concerning the present status of the experiment.[27]

Hegel assigned Bergeland the task of assembling this information. Her report, which was completed the following month, offers a good picture of the first students enrolled in the B Curriculum Experiment. There were, according to Bergeland, eighty-four students enrolled in the program, forty-one in seventh-grade and forty-three in eighth-grade. The majority of the students were of normal intellectual ability with an average I.Q. score for the group of eighty-nine. There were four students with I.Q.s over one hundred, and six children with I.Q.s between seventy and eighty, children who during this period would be classified as mentally retarded. There were in the program thirty-five children who were anywhere from a half-year to three years overage for their grade, thirty-five who were in the appropriate age for their grade, and fourteen who were a half-year to one year underage. There were forty children in the program who had repeated one or more courses, and there were nineteen children who, according to teacher judgments, had defects in ability. Of these, seven were thought to be "slow" or have "lack of judgment," and five were thought to have speech or hearing impairments or to exhibit unspecified "nervous disorders." There were also eight children in the program who, teachers felt, exhibited various behavioral problems.[28]

The modifications necessary in the regular curriculum for the Small Class Experiment were, according to Bergeland, minimal. In English, B Curriculum students studied the same content as did students in the regular classes. In comparison to children in regular classes, however, these Small Class students used books written at a lower reading level, devoted more time to reading and spelling, and took more trips to the school library. In mathematics, the teachers spent more time than they did in regular classes on the fundamental operations, used simpler and more practical word problems, and took special pains to make their directions as clear and precise as possible. Despite these changes, Bergeland maintained, the teachers of Small Classes attempted to follow the regular curriculum as much as possible. She reported that the students themselves requested that they be taught the same material as was given to students in Folwell's regular classes.

To help assure this similarity, teachers assigned to Small Classes were also assigned regular classes in the same subject at the same grade level. Bergeland was, it seems, aware of the possibility that a Small Class Experiment that departed too greatly from the regular school program could harm rather than help these children:

> Great care must be taken that children in the small classes do not feel inferior. The teachers must be optimistic and wholeheartedly a part of the program. Pupils placed in these classes must understand why they are placed there and also that there is no closed gate for them. They must understand that there is an open road into and out of the regular classes. No child should remain in the class against his will. The success of the B Curriculum program is found in the individual child's achievement, his feeling of satisfaction brought about by being "on his own," thinking independently and taking an active part in the life of the school.[29]

Bergeland concluded her report by noting that because of the B Curriculum, "it has been possible to eliminate all failure from the seventh- and eighth-grades."[30] While her judgment was ostensibly correct, the average grades she reported for the students enrolled in this program suggested a more modest assessment of the success of the B Curriculum. Of the eighty-four students enrolled in Small Classes during the 1944–1945 academic year, twenty-nine received a grade point average of C or C+, twenty-seven received an average of C– or D+, and twenty-eight received an average of D or D–. While no one really failed, only thirty-five percent of the students achieved at what might be thought of as an average level.[31] Despite these results, however, her report convinced the city's junior high school principals to recommend the extension of the B Curriculum to all of their schools beginning the following Fall.[32]

The teachers who implemented the B Curriculum in the Fall of 1946 were not, however, as certain as were Hegel or Beregland about the relationship of this innovation to the regular curriculum. Mary Beauchamp, a curriculum consultant for the city, noted that some teachers saw the Small Class Experiment as compatible with other curriculum reforms of the day and supported it. Others, however, believed that the Small Class was "just a glorified special class" for less able students and tended to view the program with skepticism.[33] A memorandum to Assistant Superintendent Robert Gilchrist from the B Curriculum Materials Committee three months earlier seemed to point to the same problem. The communication contained comments from principals concerning the efforts of their teachers to implement this curriculum proposal.

Most of the comments indicated that this was a relatively easy task requiring few, if any, changes in the regular program. Some of the comments, however, indicated that teachers were making major modifications in their courses, changes that were turning the Small Class into a remedial program. According to one of the principals, "no attempt [was] made to cover a definite course of study. Teachers have selected books and materials. [The] method of approach [was] adjusted to the groups." Another principal noted that teachers "have tried to pick and choose materials and topics suited to the abilities and interests of the groups." And finally, a third principal stated that his B Curriculum teachers were using "different books" and assigning the students "easier projects" than were his regular classroom teachers.[34] Some of these teachers seemed, like Hegel and Bergeland, to be defenders of a common curriculum for the city's children. Others, however, saw this reform as representing something different from the regular school program.

The problem was that various groups within the city

schools had different and often conflicting ideas of what the Small Class was all about. In March 1947 the B Curriculum Steering Committee met to hear reports from three of its subcommittees that were appointed to look at different aspects of the Small Class Experiment. The report of the Subcommittee on Learning Materials noted that with some slight modifications, students in the Small Classes "should have the same curriculum as other students."[35] The Policy Subcommittee, on the other hand, depicted the Small Class as a special class by describing it as "an adjustment program that will meet the needs of poor achievers such as students having poor work habits, mental and social maladjustments, physical or health handicaps, and language difficulties."[36] And similarly, the Implications Subcommittee reinforced the difference between the B Curriculum and regular classes when they recommended that Small Class students be evaluated on the basis of their attitudes, not their subject matter achievement.[37]

In the face of this conflict over the B Curriculum during its first year in operation, the city school managers decided that beginning in the Fall of 1947, they would discontinue the practice of placing a Small Class Program in each of the city's junior high schools. Instead, the administration offered junior high school principals a number of alternatives for accommodating slow-learning students. First, they could continue the existing Small Class Experiment involving separate classes of twenty students each in English, social studies, and mathematics. Second, they could serve slow-learning students in Common Learnings, a two-hour program organized around the problems of contemporary youth that students took in lieu of English and social studies. These specially designated Common Learnings classes, however, would be limited to twenty students each. Third, they could abandon the Small Class Experiment and place low-achieving students in regular Common Learnings classes, which were heterogeneously grouped, but offer them tutorial help. And fourth, they could place these students in Common Learnings classes and leave it to the teachers to help these children as far as they could.[38] They could in other words place these children in separate Small Classes or make their regular classes accessible to them. Ten of the city's junior high schools decided to continue with the Small Class Experiment. Sheridan Junior High School selected the second plan, Nokomis and Marshall the third, and Jordan the fourth.[39]

At the Summer Curriculum Workshop in July 1947, the administration appointed a committee to evaluate the relative effectiveness of these four plans for serving low-achieving students. The committee recommended that students be assessed using achievement tests in reading, mathematics, and spelling, a personality inventory, and a behavior rating scale. They also recommended that teachers should create folders for their students in which they collected other relevant information concerning their progress. In September it was decided that the evaluation be limited to the seventh-grade.[40]

The evaluation, which was conducted throughout the 1947–1948 academic year, produced inconclusive results. Those in charge of conducting the evaluation felt that neither the personality inventory nor the behavior rating scale provided much in the way of useful information. They also claimed that the achievement tests were not very sensitive to the kind of modest academic growth exhibited by the city's slow-learning students. The test results, they argued, had underestimated the true academic improvement of these students. "Many pupils," they concluded, "had made satisfactory gains."[41]

Interestingly enough, two schools that had implemented the original Small Class Experiment reached conflicting conclusions about its effectiveness. The Henry Junior/Senior High School administration lauded the B Curriculum because about fifteen of the thirty-three students enrolled in the Small Class had shown improvement. At Edison Junior/Senior High School, on the other hand, the administration reported that "standardized achievement tests gave very little evidence that the Small Class had been very beneficial."[42]

An evaluation at Nokomis Junior High School of two groups of students who were enrolled in the B Curriculum for one year and then returned to their regular classes also showed conflicting results. One group had entered the Small Class Program in the seventh-grade and moved on to regular classes in the eighth-grade. The other group had entered the Small Class Program in the eighth-grade and moved on to regular classes in the ninth-grade. The study involved a comparison of the grade point averages that these students received in their Small Classes with their grade point averages in regular classes the following year. This was accomplished by assigning each of the grades that students received a numerical score between three and minus one (A=3, B=2, C=1, D=0, F=-1). The first group, which included twenty-one students, received a mean grade point average of .57 or midway between a C and a D in their seventh-grade Small Classes and a grade point average of .14 or just a bit above a D in their eighth-grade classes. The second group of twenty-two students, however, saw a slight improvement in their grade point average. In the eighth-grade these students earned a mean grade point average of .32 or a low D. In the ninth-grade, these students earned a mean grade point average of .425, still in the D range but a bit higher. The data from Nokomis, then, provided inconsistent findings about the ability of the Small Class Experiment to improve the achievement of slow-learning students. And whatever improvement that the B Curriculum produced, it was, at best, minimal.[43]

It is not exactly clear why Minneapolis teachers held conflicting views about the Small Class Experiment or why students enrolled in Small Classes exhibited little or no improvement. One explanation may be that these students were particularly difficult to teach and to manage. Of the eleven students enrolled in the Small Class at Franklin Junior High School during the Fall 1947 term, about half had I.Q. scores in the seventies or eighties. Virtually all the students had arithmetic and reading achievement test scores that were two years behind grade level, and half the children lived in single parent families or posed discipline problems for the regular teachers.[44] These were children, it seems, who did not like school and who rarely did well when in school. They were children whom teachers did not want to teach and who did not typically respond well to the efforts of teachers.

In June 1948 the city's junior high school principals were asked to choose which of any of the four plans for teaching slow-learners they would adopt during the next academic year. Nine of them decided to place their low-achieving students in heterogeneous Common Learnings classes and to provide them with tutorial help. Three of the principals opted to continue using Small Classes, employing either the original or the Common Learnings organizational pattern. And two of the principals indicated that they had no plans for addressing the needs of their slow-learners. Of the ten schools that had originally adopted homogeneously grouped Small Classes, only Lincoln Junior High School decided to continue with that plan. Folwell Junior High School, which had initiated the B Curriculum in 1945, decided to abolish it in favor of the Common Learnings program. Mary Beauchamp viewed these choices positively, noting that it was "a very encouraging development from the point where we started—that is, of setting these students off by themselves."[45]

What Newton Hegel and Eva Bergeland envisoned as a way to make Minneapolis junior high schools more accessible to slow-learning children became, when implemented by the city's teachers, a separate and segregated class. It was, however, not all that certain that the decision to virtually abandon the Small Class Experiment was the result of any widespread belief that slow-learning students could benefit from being placed in regular classrooms. That decision was more likely the result of frustrated principals who did not know how to respond to teachers who were unwilling or unable to understand the purpose of the B Curriculum. When given the opportunity, which the equivocal results of the citywide evaluation offered them, most of these principals decided to abandon this approach to enhancing state capacity rather than trying to promote it among the city's teachers.

V.

With the virtual demise of the B Curriculum Experiment in 1948, Minneapolis did not have a single citywide initiative in place to deal with low-achieving students. Some of these children, no doubt, found their way into one of the city's special education programs. Although ostensibly designed for children who were mentally retarded, deaf, blind, orthopedically handicapped, or speech impaired, these programs also served children whose school problems were of inexplicable origin. Speech clinicians in Minneapolis, not unlike their counterparts in Atlanta, provided therapy for children whose language impairments were the result of uncertain central nervous system dysfunctions. Similarly, the city's special classes for educationally mentally retarded children enrolled students with near normal intelligence test scores who were described as slow-learners.[46]

The city did undertake some efforts that were specifically directed toward children who were academically troublesome but not handicapped. One tactic that enjoyed particular popularity during this period was the workshop. In June 1954, for example, Maynard Reynolds, Director of the Psycho-Educational Clinic at the University of Minnesota, offered a workshop on the slow-learner for the city's principals and curriculum consultants. During the morning session of the workshop, Reynolds spoke on the teaching of slow-learners, and in the afternoon a panel of principals and consultants reacted to his presentation.[47]

Demographic changes, however, would spur on more extensive efforts. Between 1950 and 1960, Minneapolis's population underwent a 7.4 percent decline from 521,718 to 482,872. During that period, the city's black population almost doubled from 6,807 to 11,785.[48] Although blacks accounted only for 2.5 percent of Minneapolis's inhabitants in 1960, their growing proportion in the population attracted the attention of the city's school managers. A 1963 planning document, which was prepared for the city by Michigan State University, noted that there was a correlation between the city's growing nonwhite population and the existence of slum neighborhoods. And such neighborhoods, the report went on to say, were breeding grounds for culturally deprived children who required an array of extra educational services, including psychological counseling, social work, and the development of remedial programs.[49]

One of the city's first attempts to respond to this population change occurred in 1962 with the creation of a program of

Remedial Reading Centers. Established in elementary schools throughout the city, the Centers were designed to provide assistance to children with near normal I.Q.s but with significant reading problems. At about the same time, South High School had set up a program similar to the B Curriculum in which entering junior high school students, who were thought to be potential dropouts, were assigned to social studies classes that were limited to twelve to fifteen students. Staffed with teachers who voiced a desire to work with low-achieving students, these classes employed a modified curriculum in which content was organized around the immediate concerns and interests of adolescents.[50] There were, in fact, several similar programs available throughout the city around this time to accommodate such students.[51]

The city's teachers were, as was the case with the B Curriculum, less enthusiastic about these efforts than were school managers. In February 1963 Kopple Friedman, a school system curriculum consultant, noted some of the questions teachers routinely raised about the effort of the city to accommodate slow-learners. Among their questions were the following: "Isn't there some place else than school where we can send slow-learners?" "If these pupils do not read the material that other pupils do, how will they be able to pass any tests?" "Are we going to water down the curriculum for them?" "What will happen to my standards?" It would appear, then, that some of the city's teachers, at least enough to capture the attention of the administration, did not want slow-learning students in their classrooms. They doubted their ability to teach these students effectively, and they believed that their presence would undermine the academic standards they had established for their other students.[52]

Despite these reservations on the part of some teachers, there were others who did try to make provisions for slow-learners. How credible their efforts were remains uncertain. In June 1964 Friedman wrote to a Northeast Junior High School teacher, Wayne Anderson, granting him permission to undertake an experiment for low-achieving eighth-graders. In his letter, he requested that Anderson make some modifications in his plan. He noted that it was appropriate for Anderson to modify the content of his social studies course so that it was more interesting to slow-learners. Yet he thought the topics that Anderson had proposed, one of them being home maintenance, needed to be related to the study of history. The administration, Friedman stated, "would have preferred that you started with something in history that could provide a lesson related to one of your topics and then lead to that topic as an outcome." Home maintenance, he thought, could be an appropriate topic if it were linked to the study of the history of the family.

Friedman also noted that Assistant Superintendent Adner Heggerston had wanted Anderson to do more planning for the course than he had originally proposed. "When I told him, as you told me, that you would start by going into class the first day and merely talking, he was not at all satisfied. He feels that there must be some definite plans."[53]

What began in the early 1930s as an effort to accommodate low-achieving children by reducing class size and rendering the curriculum more practical had, it seems, three decades later gone virtually nowhere. For the most part the responses of teachers during the early 1960s to the presence of low-achieving students in their classes, a mix of skepticism, vexation, and opposition, were about the same as the responses of teachers to the B Curriculum Experiment. The efforts of Minneapolis school managers to accommodate low-achieving children seemed to have reached a dead end. It would take, as we shall now see, a reconceptualization of the problem using a medicalized discourse to renew their state-building efforts.

VI.

In 1957 the Minnesota Legislature amended its existing permissive special education law to require that the state's school districts provide instruction for handicapped children who were orthopedically disabled, deaf, blind, speech impaired, and educably mentally retarded. As part of the bill, the Legislature expanded the definition of mental retardation to include not only children with I.Q.s below 80 but children who were emotionally disturbed, who exhibited special behavior problems, or "who for any other reason need special instruction."[54]

Such an all-encompassing definition of mental retardation would, as it turned out, extend special education to a wide array of the state's children. Virtually any child who was in danger of failure was in fact eligible for services.[55] To differentiate these students from those traditionally labeled mentally retarded, Minnesota began during the early 1960s to refer to this new group of handicapped children as having special learning disabilities. To see how this expansion occurred, we need to look beyond the city's public schools to the work of the Kenny Rehabilitation Institute.

The Institute was established in 1942 in Minneapolis at the urging of Sister Elizabeth Kenny to promote the approach to treating infantile paralysis which she had first developed as a nurse in Australia and was then practicing in the city's hospitals. During the early 1960s, staff members at the Institute were engaged in research, similar to that which we discussed in chapter three, on the central nervous system correlates of school learning problems. In 1962 Paul Ellwood, an Institute neurologist, received a grant from the U.S. Public Health Service to develop in conjunction with the Minneapolis Public Schools a diagnostic and treatment program for children whose school problems were the result of "subtle neurological and sensory disorders."[56]

The first phrase of the project involved the evaluation of approximately thirty-five children with learning and behavior problems. Part of this group was composed of children referred by school social workers because they exhibited a discrepancy between their achievement and intelligence or because they were hyperactive, withdrawn, or inattentive. The other part of the group was composed of children who had been referred to the city's existing special education programs and had just been placed in a special setting or were awaiting placement.

Once selected, the children were administered a natural sleep electroencephalogram and then placed for four weeks of observation in a special class at Madison School under the direction of Harriet Burns, a Minneapolis special education teacher assigned to the project. In their first week at Madison, the children were observed and given a pediatric neurological examination and a psychometric battery composed of intelligence, achievement, and perceptual-motor tests. At the conclusion of this testing, the Kenny research team provided a provisional assessment of each child's problems and developed an individual treatment program. During the next three weeks, Burns implemented these individualized programs. In addition, some of the children were placed on drug therapy, involving one or more stimulant or anticonvulsant drugs. Besides providing direct services to children, the research team developed a parent education program to involve the families of these children in treatment efforts.[57] Of the children who participated in the project, the research team concluded that about half "show abnormal findings suggestive of central nervous system pathology."[58]

In initiating this project, Ellwood, Burns, and the other members of the research team were interested in the applicability of the neurological impairment hypothesis to children who were not routinely thought of as being handicapped. They had wanted but were unable to include in their research, children enrolled in the city's Remedial Reading Centers.[59] The following year, however, they were able to evaluate a group of remedial reading students and compare their performance with their initial group of neurologically impaired children. They found that these children with reading difficulties exhibited a "higher incidence of neurological abnormalities." Unlike the initial experimental group, however, these children showed greater anxiety, were more inhibited, and were more easily controlled.[60] The conclusions of the Kenny project were, of course, no less problematic than the findings of Strauss and Werner two decades earlier. As Burns noted in reflecting back on her work, only an autopsy could definitively reveal the existence of brain injury.[61] Minneapolis's school managers were, nonetheless, impressed by the findings of the Kenny research team. Evelyn Deno, Director of Special Education, noted that the results were "intriguing and, of course, potentially highly significant in its potentialities for financing of special services." She went on to point out that if children in the city's Remedial

Reading Centers were organically impaired, as Ellwood and his colleagues suggested, then these children would be eligible for placement in special education.[62]

The concern that surfaced in Atlanta during the early 1960s about neurologically induced learning problems in intellectually normal children was also to be found during this period in Minneapolis. Writing in the *Minneapolis Tribune* in October 1964, Mike Hull noted the case of a second-grade boy, Dick, who when asked to read orally by his teacher began disrupting the class. Hull noted that this child could have had an emotional upsetness of one sort or another. It was also possible, according to Hull, that Dick was brain damaged.[63] Another story in the same issue reported on Evelyn Deno's speech to the Minnesota Association for Brain-Injured Children. According to Deno, "the blind, deaf and crippled children in Minneapolis are just about 100 percent taken care of." She felt, however, that the city's neurologically impaired children required additional special educational services.[64]

Taken together, Minnesota's broadened definition of mental retardation, the work of the Kenny Institute, and an increasing public awareness about so-called neurologically impaired children, had the effect of transforming the discourse that Minneapolis school managers had used to talk about low-achievement. What had been conceptualized as learning difficulties of diffuse or even indefinite origins had become a distinct neurological impairment. And the special class that Burns had established at Madison School became a model for a new bureaucratic strategy of accommodating low-achieving students, the special learning disabilities or SLD class. In 1962 Minneapolis established its first special learning disabilities or SLD class at Emerson Elementary School. During the next eight years, these classes would be established in virtually all the city's seventy elementary schools and in eleven of its seventeen junior high schools.[65]

The establishment of SLD classes also affected the city's Remedial Reading Centers. The finding of the Kenny research team that a number of the children attending the Centers were neurologically impaired led some to question the need for a remedial reading program. In May 1967 Mildred Carlson, an elementary school curriculum consultant, wrote Assistant Superintendent Rodney Tillman to ask whether the Remedial Reading Centers were duplicating the work of the city's SLD classes. There was the need, she thought, to coordinate the work of the two programs. Toward that end, Carlson offered three solutions. First, the existing practice of placing Remedial Reading Centers or SLD tutors in some of the city's schools could be continued. Second, SLD tutors or remedial reading teachers could be added to each elementary school until all the schools had one specialist or the other. And third, SLD tutors could be assigned to teach special education students exclusively, while remedial reading teachers could work specifically with children exhibiting reading problems.[66]

Rather than continue to offer two programs, however, the administration decided to merge them beginning in the Fall of 1967. The teachers who operated the city's fifteen Remedial Reading Centers would be reclassified as special learning disability resource teachers or SLDR teachers. Other schools would be assigned SLDR tutors. In effect what had been a remedial reading program had become a program for the learning disabled.[67] At its February 1968 meeting, the Board of Education formally approved the merger of these two programs with the understanding that SLDR teachers were also qualified to teach reading.[68]

By uniting these two enterprises, Minneapolis's school managers had under the rubric of learning disabilities created a single special education program that served a diverse variety of low-achieving students. Some were neurologically impaired while others were socially maladjusted, emotionally disturbed, or simply academically delayed.[69] In creating this program, Minneapolis educators were subscribing to a view of learning disabilities that was broader than the definition that the National Advisory Committee on Handicapped Children proposed in 1968.[70] Nonetheless, it was a definition that recognized the diversity of children for which a modern, urban school system had to make provision. By the middle of the 1960s, those children who three decades earlier had been referred to as slow-learners or backward and were seen as the responsibility of regular classroom teachers had been transformed into learning disabled children who were the responsibility of special educators.

Examining the efforts of Minneapolis's school managers to accommodate children with learning difficulties reveals, in ways that our study of Atlanta did not, the intricacies surrounding this kind of state-building. The city's school managers could not simply devise a bureaucratic strategy that they thought best for handling difficult to teach children. They had to deal with teachers who were often skeptical, if not downright opposed to the B Curriculum Experiment. Initially their opposition transformed an effort to preseve common schooling into a separate and segregated class. Ultimately, their opposition spelled the demise of this reform. Second, there was a critical interplay between the discourse used to frame the problem of low-achievement and state-building. The work of the Kenny Institute to transform low-achievement into a neurological impairment allowed for creation of the SLD class, which did not depend on the involvement of the city's regular classroom teachers for its success. And once established, the SLD class served to extend the reach of this medicalized discourse to encompass an increasing array of learning difficulties, including reading problems, social maladjustment, and emotional disturbance.

VII.

The establishment of special classes for children with learning difficulties, I argued in earlier chapters, was guided by contradictory goals. It was never clear if the impetus for these programs was to help children with learning difficulties, or to contain the presumed threat that these children posed to the work of the regular class. The conflicts that some parents had with the city's school managers over the Minneapolis learning disabilities program signals that here, too, the effort was plagued with contradictions.[71] In April 1971 Michael Bress wrote Superintendent John Davis and the members of the Board of Education about the city's services for learning disabled children. Bress and his wife, he noted, had recently attended a meeting of the Minnesota Association for Children with Learning Disabilities (ACLD), the successor organization to the Association for the Brain-Injured Children. They had hoped to question the invited speaker, Harriet Burns, who was in charge of the city SLD program. Those who attended the meeting, according to Bress, had wanted Burns to, in his words, "explain to us why the Minneapolis schools are failing to meet their statutory obligation to educate the handicapped but educable child." Burns, however, did not attend the meeting. Her failure to attend without canceling was, as Bress saw it, "sadly indicative of the Minneapolis school administration's lack of concern for the child with learning disabilities."

Bress then went on to talk about the problems that his third grade son, Robert, had encountered at Kenwood School. There was, he claimed, no diagnostic services available in the city to determine what was wrong with his son. When Robert was in the first grade, Bress had to pay $75 to have a private psychologist evaluate him. The psychologist had recommended that Robert be given five hours of tutoring a week. Since the school, again according to Bress, did not provide tutors, he had to hire a private tutor at $80 a month who was able to offer Robert only three hours a week of help. Bress was not only upset by what he believed was the city's failure to provide needed services to his son, he was also angered by the treatment Robert had received from his first-grade teacher. He noted that although the tutor felt that Robert was "making great progress in reading and self-confidence," his teacher "had branded him as ignorant and lazy." Bress thought that a disability, which he claimed affected ten to fifteen percent of school children, deserved more careful and caring attention.[72]

Burns's failure to attend the Association's meeting was, as it turned out, unintentional. The ACLD had extended an invitation to Burns to speak to its members, but her appearance for the particular meeting that the Bresses attended had not been confirmed.[73] When Davis was informed of this, he directed his assistant, Marvin Trammel to write Bress and "in a sharp direct way indicate the reason [for Burns's absence] and suggest that in the future before he write such a letter, he discover the facts in the matter."[74] After talking with the school system's Special Education Department, Trammel prepared a letter challenging each of Bress's complaints, which was sent out under Davis's signature. In the letter, Davis noted that Minneapolis operated a state-approved program for learning disabled children and that the city was expanding its psychological testing and tutoring services. He disagreed with Bress's incidence figures, claiming instead that only one to two percent of school children were learning disabled. The problem, according to Davis, was not a lack of services in Minneapolis. Rather, there was no record that Bress's son had been referred to the special learning disabilities program for an evaluation. Davis closed his letter by noting that there was no clear evidence that Robert's first-grade teacher had made the comments that Bress had attributed to her.[75]

Five months later, Bress wrote back to Davis, this time, however, in a more conciliatory tone. He noted that after he had sent his initial letter, the availability of services increased and teacher attitudes at Kenwood seemed to improve. Nevertheless, he still took issue with some of Davis's comments. He stated that Robert had been tested by a psychologist at the University of Minnesota and that the results of this assessment had been reported to his teacher, to the counselor, and to the principal. He commented to Davis in this vein that perhaps there was some problem with staff communications at the school.

Bress also challenged Davis's estimate of the learning disabled population. If one to two percent was, as Davis indicated, the correct incidence figure, then the single learning disabilities teacher who was assigned to Kenwood last year would have been sufficient. Yet in Robert's second-grade class, seven out of the twenty-seven students enrolled were learning disabled, but only a few of them actually received any assistance. He went on to note that some parents had placed their learning disabled children in private schools, while others had left Minneapolis for better public school programs in the suburbs. Bress stated that, in fact, fifteen percent of the children in the Minneapolis Public Schools were receiving special education for learning disabilities. As a solution, he suggested that perhaps the parents of learning disabled children in the same school could pay a tuition charge to support the assignment of an additional special education teacher to that school.[76]

Later that same month, Richard Johnson, Director of Minneapolis's Special Education Department, wrote to Bress. He noted that Bress had not followed proper procedures concerning his son's evaluation, because he had not provided the school with a copy of the test results until the end of the academic year. In the interim, the school had in fact determined that Robert's condition was not sufficiently severe to warrant tutoring services. Johnson then went on to address the question of the incidence of learning disabilities. Although incidence figures were, he stated, "quite unreliable," it was true that there were last year more learning disabled children at Kenwood than could be served by the school's single learning disabilities teacher. Johnson stated that this condition would continue until the Minnesota legislature appropriated sufficient funds to support special education.

Johnson took issue with Bress's claim that parents were withdrawing their children from the Minneapolis schools in hopes of finding better services in private schools or in the suburbs. He argued that there were no private schools in close proximity to Minneapolis that offered special programs for the learning disabled and that no suburban school system spent as much on learning disabled children as did Minneapolis. He concluded his letter by noting that it would be a violation of state law for the school district to collect money from parents to support additional teachers for learning disabled students.[77]

Although it might appear at first glance that school managers were unresponsive to Bress's charges, he was actually successful in bringing some changes to the services provided for learning disabled children, at least at Kenwood School. In October of the following year, Grace Bress wrote to Ann Danahy, Kenwood's Principal, and to the members of the Board of Education to thank them for the changes that had been made at the school since her husband's initial complaint. In her letter to Danahy, she thanked the Principal for both providing additional tutoring for her son and for establishing workshops to make the school's teachers aware of the problem of learning disabilities. She was particularly grateful, she concluded, for the letter that Danahy had sent to parents indicating the school's commitment to provide educational excellence for all its students.[78]

At just about the same time that the administration was resolving its dispute with Bress, the city school managers became embroiled in another parental conflict. In the Spring of 1971, a Mrs. Dabrowski contacted Superintendent Davis to request that the city pay part of the tuition for her learning disabled son, Craig, to attend Breck School, an independent day school in Minneapolis. Craig had attended kindergarten and first grade at Hiawatha School, but was not doing well, because of a combination of learning and behavior problems. At their own expense, his parents had transferred Craig to Breck for the second and third grade where a structured curriculum and small classes were helping him to earn a B or better in all his subjects. Unable to bear the tuition costs, the Dabrowskis returned Craig to Hiawatha for the fourth grade where he again began to experience difficulties. A pediatric diagnostic team from the Kenny Institute that had evaluated Craig felt that his problems were the result of the lack of structure in his class at Hiawatha and recommended that he be placed in a private school such as Breck.[79]

The problem, according to Jerry Gross of Minneapolis's Special Education Department, was that the city had never applied to the state for the kind of tuition reimbursement that the Dabrowskis were requesting, nor had the state ever offered such tuition assistance to any other public school. The Dabrowkis could, he noted, appeal to the Commissioner of Education for tuition assistance, but that it was his judgment that such an allocation would represent "a misuse of state funds."[80]

In September, Associate Superintendent James Kennedy wrote to the Dabrowskis to report that public funds could not be used to pay for Craig's tuition at Breck. He then went on to note that Craig's evaluation at the Kenny Institute found that his problems were not due to learning disabilities but to behavior problems. And there were two appropriate public school placements for a child with such difficulties. There was a structured class at Keewaydin School, and a new program for children with behavior disorders that had just been established at Madison School.[81]

Although the Dabrowskis did enroll Craig at Breck at their own expense, they did, early in January of the following year, hire an attorney, Walter Duffy, to see if they could obtain a reimbursement from the city.[82] Kennedy referred the issue to the school system's attorney, Norman Newhall. He, in turn, wrote Duffy to indicate that the kind of reimbursement sought by the Dabrowskis was not one that the city could or would make.[83] There is no record that the Dabrowskis pursued the matter any further.

Although neither the Bresses nor the Dabrowskis were completely victorious in their struggles with the city, their complaints did have an effect. In October 1972 Superintendent Davis informed the Board that a highly structured program for the severely learning disabled was to be established in the Fall at Armitage School. The class was limited to fourteen severely impaired children and would provide each of them with a totally individualized program.[84] From what we have considered thus far in this volume, one may well wonder how much of a solution a new special class was to the kind of problems encountered by the Bresses or the Dabrowskis.

VIII.

Some parents, however, were never satisfied by the accommodations that the public schools offered their learning disabled children. Instead of challenging school managers as did the Bresses or the Dabrowskis, they chose to abandon the public schools and turned to private philanthropy for help. In 1971 a number of prominent families from Minneapolis, St. Paul, and the surrounding suburbs, frustrated in their own attempts to secure adequate public school services for their learning disabled children, joined together to establish a private school. The driving force behind the effort was Thomas Hartzell, President of Hartzell Manufacturing Company. Earlier in his career, while living in Denver, Hartzell was unable to find an appropriate public school program for his learning disabled son Bob. Although the child had an I.Q. of 140, he had failed all his eighth-grade subjects. Hartzell sent Bob to a boarding school in the Northeast for a year. Aided by his private school experience, Bob returned to the Denver Public Schools, graduated from high school, and was presently doing well as a student at the University of Denver.[85] As one might expect, Hartzell had been interested for quite some time in the problems of learning disabled children. During the 1960s, he had established a foundation that supported the development of programs for learning disabled children in St. Paul and in a small suburban district near Minneapolis.[86]

The school opened in 1972 in the suburb of Hopkins and was named the Groves Learning Center in honor of Franklin Groves, grandfather of a learning disabled child, a major financial contributor to the project, and the head of a large Minneapolis construction company.[87] As a new enterprise that was short on financial resources, the Groves Center had to charge an annual tuition of $3800, which was beyond the means of many parents who wished to send their children to the school. What the Center's Board of Directors hoped, however, was that those school districts that did not have their own learning disabilities program would place their students at Groves and pay the tuition.[88] The Board, as events turned out, was never that successful in convincing public school managers to place their students in Groves in lieu of establishing their own programs. In the school's first year of operation, area public schools were paying tuition for about eight of the thirty-four students enrolled. Five years later, they were supporting about twenty-eight of the seventy students enrolled. Thereafter, public school tuition payments declined, and by 1982 public schools were paying tuition only for about six of the Center's approximately one hundred students.[89]

Sending their students to Groves, it seems, placed school districts in an untenable position. In 1974 Warren MacFarlane requested the State Commissioner of Education to order the Minnetonka Public Schools, a suburban district west of Minneapolis, to reimburse him for the tuition he was paying to place his learning disabled son at Groves. MacFarlane had originally withdrawn his son from Minnetonka because he believed that the district did not offer an appropriate learning disabilities program. An initial settlement was worked out in which the Minnetonka Board of Education would reimburse MacFarlane for thirty-five percent of the $4,000 annual tuition or $1400. The Board, however, changed its mind and refused to honor the settlement. School Board member John Adams pointed out that if the district paid MacFarlane, it would be admitting that it did not have an adequate program.

The Board decided to challenge the Commissioner's ruling in court, appealing first to the Hennepin County Superior Court and then to the Minnesota Supreme Court. Both courts ruled in favor of the Commissioner and ordered Minnetonka to pay the child's tuition for the 1974–1975 academic year and to develop an appropriate educational program for him for the following year. Minnetonka complied and MacFarlane returned his child to the public schools. As late as 1976, however, MacFarlane was still dissatisfied with Minnetonka's efforts and filed a $160,000 law suit against the district and appealed the ruling of a state hearing officer, which held that Minnetonka was offering an appropriate educational program for the learning disabled.[90]

Placing a child in a private school was not only financially costly to a school district. It set the stage for parental conflicts over educational quality, which a public school had virtually no chance of winning. When faced, then, with the choice of sending a child to Groves and paying the tuition or establishing their own program, most school districts, seeking to avoid the kind of problems that haunted Minnetonka, chose the latter alternative. In Minneapolis's adjacent suburbs, then, it was not the public schools but private philanthropy that took the initiative in establishing programs for learning disabled children. And this initiative, like its counterpart in Atlanta, would act to propel forward the efforts of public school managers to create programs for the learning disabled. And as was the case in Atlanta, the result would be a dual system, one private for those who could pay the tuition and the other public for those who could not.

By 1970, some forty years after Minneapolis first began its remedial education efforts, it was still unclear that the city's school managers had come to grips with the presence of low-achieving children in their schools. They had not been able to reconcile the contradictory purposes that appeared to direct their efforts to accommodate children with learning difficulties. Writing to Superintendent John Davis in May 1970 to resign his teaching position at the Madison School SLD program, Peter DeVaney noted the absence of the kind of resources that would make Madison accessible to children with learning problems. The program lacked enough teachers to supervise the reintegration of students into regular classrooms, sufficient supplies, and the services of a psychologist for conducting evaluations. The SLD program, he stated, "will become stagnant, because it seems to us that the administration neither knows what needs we are serving, nor is interested in helping us to serve these needs." If present practices were to continue, he cautioned, the city's SLD program would become a "dumping ground" for low-achieving children.[91]

It was not only Minneapolis's school managers who were uncertain about the accessibility they should provide to children with learning difficulties. The city itself, as an exchange of letters in the *Minneapolis Tribune* would suggest, was divided on this issue. In June 1969 Jane Rachner wrote the editor of the *Tribune* concerning what she claimed was the myth of dyslexia. This term did not really refer to an individual disability. Rather, it was "a euphemism for what happens when school instruction is so confusing that intelligent school children cannot benefit from it." The cause of this problem, according to Rachner, was the devotion of the nation's teachers to modern educational theory, or as she put it "developmentalism," which had for some time monopolized the thinking of faculties of schools of education. What was required if schools were to improve, Rachner implied, was to abandon "Dick and Jane" in favor of a more traditional curriculum.[92]

Two weeks later, Beatrice Linn wrote to the editor to challenge Rachner's claims. That schools often embrace this fad or another in place of a sound curriculum, she argued, does not mean that there is no such thing as dyslexia. She suggested that those such as Rachner who doubt the existence of this disability should try to teach a child who has no sequence or sense of direction or sees things backwards.[93] Not unlike Minneapolis's school managers, its citizenry was unable to reconcile their desire to have a system of schooling that was accessible to all children with their fear about the presence in regular classrooms of children with learning difficulties.

IX.

In this chapter we have examined the almost half-century attempt of Minneapolis's school managers to make provisions for children with learning difficulties. During this period, the city school managers introduced a variety of bureaucratic strategies to accommodate these children. Initially, they attempted to make these provisions without radically differentiating the curriculum for low-achieving children. During the 1930s, they modified the curriculum to introduce more practical course content. A decade later, they introduced the B Curriculum or Small Class Experiment, which assigned slow-learning junior high school students to classes that were half the size of regular junior high school classes. Despite their smaller enrollments, these classes did cover virtually the same content that was offered in the regular school program. During the 1960s, however, the emergence of a medicalized discourse for talking about low achievement led the city's school managers to take a different approach. They abandoned attempts to accommodate these children in regular classrooms and instead created special learning disabilities or SLD classes to accommodate these children.

Notwithstanding the different state-building strategies which these school managers embraced during these years, they were unable to reconcile the contradictory goals to which their efforts seemed directed. The creators of the B Curriculum Experiment were defenders of the the principal of common schooling and sought to minimize the differences between this reform and the regular classroom. The city's teachers, however, did not share this view. For the most part, they neither understood the program nor supported it. In the end, they transformed the Small Class into exactly what it was not designed to be, a separate and segregated remedial program. By and large, the city's teachers had little interest in accommodating low-achieving children in their classes. As they saw it, teaching such children required them to lower their standards and dilute their curriculum. In short, it interfered with their ability to teach their more able students. If these teachers had their way, they would send children with learning difficulties elsewhere.

Taken together, the work of the Kenny Institute, the establishment of the SLD classes, and the merging of these classes with the Remedial Reading Centers would ensure that low-achieving children or the learning disabled, as they were now called, would be accommodated in separate and segregated settings apart from regular classrooms. Yet this strategy was ultimately no more successful in accommodating children with learning difficulties than was the B Curriculum experiment. If we can believe the parents of these children, it was a program that seemed to offer the learning disabled little in the way of services or assistance. If it did anything, it seemed to drive many of these students out of public education and into private schooling. In the end, it brought private philanthropy onto the scene, which had the effect, as it did in Atlanta, of creating new and more permanent barriers to common schooling.

Epilogue: At-Risk Children and
the Common School Ideal

At the beginning of this book, I argued that the joint effort of public school managers and private philanthropy throughout this century to provide for children with learning difficulties can be seen as the nation's first crusade for the education of at-risk children. The preceding five chapters have been devoted to exploring the events surrounding that movement from the creation of the first public school programs for backward children at the turn of the twentieth century to the appearance on the scene of learning disabilities during the 1960s.

Early on in their attempt to provide for these children, school managers established an implicit accord among themselves and their philanthropic collaborators, which involved a recalibration of the mid-nineteenth-century common school ideal. According to this reconstituted ideal, public schools would be accessible to all children. Once inside the school, however, these children would not necessarily enjoy a shared educational experience. Rather they would be channeled to an array of remedial and special education programs, which were made possible by the emergence of a medicalized discourse for talking about childhood learning difficulties. We have already examined the evolution of this medicalized discourse from its initial formulation as backwardness to its most recent manifestation as learning disabilities. In two case studies, involving Atlanta and Minneapolis, I explored how school managers used this medicalized discourse to enhance their administrative capacities for dealing with low-achieving children. In this epilogue I will consider what the historical interpretation I have thus far developed tells us about contemporary efforts to educate at-risk children.

II.

The increasing interest of educators in the problems of at-risk children during the late 1980s and early 1990s, not unlike the concerns voiced on behalf of first backward and then learning disabled students, can be tied to ongoing societal and economic changes. The interplay during these years of three such shifts—a heightening of racial and ethnic conflicts, a changing international economy marked in this country by the decline in relatively high-paying manufacturing jobs and their replacement by lower paying service occupations, and an increasing poverty rate—have undermined the position and status of the nation's families and their children.[1]

In its 1989 report, the U.S. House of Representatives Select Committee on Children, Youth, and Families painted a rather dispiriting picture of the impact that such changes have had on these groups:

> The most profound influence on American families has been the mounting economic pressures which have diminished their resources and made more children more vulnerable. The combined effects of persistently high rates of poverty, declining earnings, underemployment, and single parenting have made childhood far more precarious and less safe for millions of American children.[2]

The report itself details an array of indicators that taken together point to a deterioration in the well-being of children and families. Between 1970 and 1985, the median family income of children, when adjusted for inflation, has declined some $1700 from $29,943 to $28,210. Since 1985, income has increased slightly, but remains below the 1970 figure. During the same period the rate of childhood poverty has increased from about fifteen percent of all children to a bit over twenty percent. And again, during these years, the percentage of children living in female-headed single households, the families most likely to live in poverty, has increased from about eight percent to fourteen percent.[3]

These changes, just as those accompanying the emergence of a market economy in the years around the turn of the century, have had an impact on childhood learning and school achievement. About one-quarter of the nation's twenty-eight million 10–17-year-olds are behind the expected grade for their age. A 1985 study by the Center for Educational Statistics, which compared the number of the nation's high school graduates that year with the number entering high school as freshman four years earlier, indicated a dropout rate of twenty-nine percent. Fourteen percent of all adolescents are functionally illiterate. In assessments of mathematics and science achievement, American thirteen-year-olds scored near or at the bottom in comparison with their peers from other industrialized nations. And according to a 1985 report from the National Assessment of Educational Progress, only eleven percent of the nation's thirteen year olds were sufficiently proficient at reading to understand written material of a complex nature.[4]

Early twentieth-century school managers, I have argued, established special classes to enhance their administrative capacity to cope with the larger and more diverse student enrollments that accompanied the nation's shift to a market economy. Similarly, the appearance on the scene of public school programs for at-risk students may signal the beginning of state-building efforts on the part today's school managers. Like their turn-of-the-century counterparts, they are attempting to augment their ability to manage low-achieving children.

The same contradictory impulses that have plagued programs for children with learning difficulties throughout this century are evident in current efforts to accommodate at-risk children. Proponents of these initiatives are often unclear as to whether they want to focus their attention on just the at-risk population or on improving education for all children.[5] Those who wish to attend solely to at-risk children tend, for the most part, to propose differentiated programs. Some, including various forms of individualized instruction and tutoring—Upward Bound, the Job Corps, and numerous Chapter One projects— represent recycled special programs from the compensatory education efforts of the 1960s.[6]

Others are apparently new, but they too rely on offering at-risk children something different from what is provided to more able students. These differentiated programs can involve the introduction of special curricula, such as basic life skills, that provide these children with capabilities that they often lack. If at-risk children are explicitly taught, among other things, how to relate appropriately to their peers, how to make decisions, how to avoid intimidation, and how to assert themselves, they can, according to advocates of this curricular offering, attain the kind of social competence that typically characterizes academically successful youth.[7]

Another approach to differentiating the curriculum for at-risk students involves the establishment of alternative schools and schools-within-schools. Typically these alternative institutions are smaller, and allow for more intimate relationships among students and faculty. They provide an environment that is designed to nurture psychological well-being. And they offer a curriculum thought to be more relevant to the interests and abilities of at-risk children. Such schools can serve to link academic course work to career preparation. And they can, with the inclusion of courses in such areas as media technology, computer applications, and photography, emphasize the kind of experiential learning often ignored by regular schools. Finally, these alternative schools can serve a particular at-risk population, say American Indians or adolescent mothers.[8]

There are, however, proposals that depart from our long-standing reliance on segregating low-achieving students. Some call for the creation of health clinics in or adjacent to schools. They would offer all students a variety of services, including routine medical examinations, care for less severe illnesses and accidents, counseling on substance abuse and pregnancy prevention, and referrals to specialists. Since, however, untreated medical problems often cause the academic and behavioral difficulties that place students at-risk, such clinics would be particularly beneficial to those children whose families lack health insurance and cannot afford private medical care.[9]

Other proposals are directed to the school's curricular and instructional programs. As one phase of its New Futures Initiative, the Annie E. Casey Foundation is currently supporting a five-year effort at curriculum reform in a number of smaller American cities with the intent of enhancing the school experience and future success of at-risk students. In its Dayton, Ohio, project, two middle schools introduced a clustering arrangement in which teachers in English, reading, mathematics, social studies, and science were placed in a single team and assigned a group of 120 to 150 students. Each teaching team was provided authority to establish its own grouping practices, to alter the existing class schedule, and to integrate their subjects around certain common and interdisciplinary themes. In Little Rock, Arkansas, a similar effort at clustering in that city's middle schools resulted in the creation of an integrated unit on violence that included instruction in English, social studies, and mathematics.

Although this and similar reforms are directed toward restructuring the schools for all students, New Futures proponents believe that they are especially helpful to at-risk children. Clustering provides a two-pronged strategy for placing teachers in a better position to recognize and provide for the academic and other difficulties that can place children at-risk. First, the members of each of these teaching teams are assigned a common planning time to allow them, among other things, to talk together to learn more about their students and their needs. Second, the relatively small size of these teams and their extensive interaction allows for more sustained and personal relationships between student and teachers.

Curriculum integration, the other key feature of this clustering arrangement, can result in a richer curriculum that is more appealing to difficult to teach children. The interdisciplinary units which the Dayton teachers created did not emphasize the drill and practice and rote memorization that has throughout this century been so much a part of the programs offered to difficult to teach students. Rather, the units they created sought to cultivate problem-solving and other higher order thinking skills.[10]

Craig Heller, a biologist from Stanford University, has designed a two-year interdisciplinary life science course for the middle schools. He also recognizes the value of curriculum integration for at-risk children. Known as Hum Bio, the course brought together disciplinary content about biology with material on such health-related topics as diet, substance abuse, and adolescent sexual development. It is a strategy, he argues, that makes the curriculum a vehicle for conveying the kind of useful information that all children, and especially those in danger of failure, need. An integrated curriculum, Heller goes on to say, offers more opportunity for student success. Children whose weakness in a single subject may consign them to failure in a traditional discipline-centered curriculum can in an interdisciplinary course often find some phase or topic that attracts their interest and builds on their strengths.[11]

One of the most extensive efforts to accommodate at-risk children without segregation is the accelerated schools project undertaken by Henry Levin and his associates at Stanford University. Accelerated schools, Levin argues, are educational institutions dedicated to the enhancement of learning for all children where teachers have a decision-making role in the school's operation, where administrators are facilitators rather than managers, and where parents are active participants in the education of their children. With respect to curricular and instructional practices, Levin and his associates appear to take their cues not from remedial programs but from those for the gifted and talented. Accelerated schools offer an enriched, common program for all students that, among other things, involves children in the use of higher order cognitive processes and problem-solving, encourages creative thinking, integrates the teaching of language throughout the curriculum, and provides for experiential learning.[12]

III.

Despite the conflicting goals that appear to guide current programs for at-risk children, there are indications of a coming sea change in our long-standing views about educating children with learning difficulties. It is a transformation in our thinking on this score that has the potential for resolving the contradictions that have plagued the efforts of school managers throughout this century to accommodate such children. One indicator of this shift is the widespread criticism that educational researchers currently direct at curriculum differentiation. The establishment of special classes for low-achieving children has been, as I noted in chapter two, one phase of the larger effort on the part of early twentieth-century school managers to differentiate the curriculum. Proposals that call for the creation of special programs for those at-risk represent a modern expression of this same impulse to sort children into separate and distinct courses of study. The problems with differentiation are that it fails to enhance the educational achievement of students, except for those who are placed in the highest tracks, leads to the disproportionate placement of poor and minority group children in lower-level classes, and has a negative impact on the overall improvement of educational quality. In short, it is a long-standing practice that has done more to exacerbate the problems of American public schooling than to resolve them.[13]

Our most recent round of educational reform, the so-called excellence movement, has been particularly unkind to curriculum differentiation. Almost uniformly, the array of reports and proposals emanating from this movement have called for the introduction of a common, academically oriented curriculum for all students, and the elimination, or at least reduction, of existing differentiated programs.[14] As the most prominent sponsors of this campaign see it, a common, academic curriculum built on the disciplines of knowledge offers the best education for all American youth. It provides the best model for conveying to children their cultural heritage, the best background for participating in democratic politics, and the best preparation for life and work in a technologically advanced society. Curriculum differentiation, they go on to say, legitimates the creation of nonacademic courses of study that lack rigor. Further, they argue, this practice is routinely used to segregate poor and minority group children from their peers, thereby consigning them to an inferior education and a subordinate place in adult society. These reformers are not opposed to some informal and temporary in-class grouping arrangements to accommodate the ability and skill differences that exist among children. They insist, however, that despite the use of different pedagogy to teach children of varying abilities, the content of education should remain the same for all children.[15] Curriculum differentiation is certainly a common feature of today's schools. Yet current criticisms of this practice suggest that we may be about ready to rethink this taken-for-granted scheme for accommodating diverse students.

IV.

Another harbinger of an approaching change in our understanding of learning difficulties has been the attack, beginning in the early 1970s and continuing today, on segregated special education. In a series of civil suits in federal and state courts during this decade, advocates of disabled children questioned in virtually the same way as had the NAACP lawyers in the 1954 case of *Brown v. the Board of Education* the constitutionality of excluding children, in this case disabled children, from the public schools.[16] Among the issues raised in these suits was the appropriateness of placing these children in special classes and other separate settings. In the majority of these cases, as it turned out, the courts ruled against segregation, arguing that the most suitable placement for most of these children was the regular classroom.[17]

Coincidental with these legal challenges were legislative efforts to ensure that disabled children had access to the nation's public schools. In a series of amendments to the Elementary and Secondary Education Act enacted between 1966 and the passage of the Education for All Handicapped Children Act

(Public Law 94–142) in 1975, Congress mandated that virtually all the nation's disabled children be guaranteed a free, public education. Among the issues raised in this legislation was the placement of disabled children once they were admitted to the public schools. Not surprisingly, Congress took a position in favor of integration and mandated that all disabled children be educated in the so-called least restrictive environment. Although this provision did appear to greatly restrict the ability of school managers to remove handicapped children from regular classrooms, it did not abolish segregated placements. Rather, the provision required that the states establish a "continuum of alternative placements" for handicapped children, which included the regular classroom, special classes and schools, and an array of nonschool settings.[18] Public schools under this provision were to place disabled children in environments that provided them with an appropriate education while maximizing their contact with their nonhandicapped peers. For many disabled children, the least restrictive placement was the regular classroom. For others, however, it was a separate classroom or school or even a residential setting.

Neither the legal challenges to the exclusion of handicapped children from the public schools and certainly not the least restrictive environment provision of P.L. 94–142 abolished the segregation of disabled children. In 1976, the year before P.L. 94–142 was implemented, about sixty-seven percent of all handicapped children and about eighty percent of learning disabled children spent some time, although we do not know precisely how much, in regular classrooms. Six years later, in 1982, the percentages were virtually unchanged.[19]

Early on, there were critics who recognized the limitations of the least restrictive environment provision. In an April 1974 letter to the House Subcommittee on Education, which was then considering the series of amendments that would become P.L. 94–142, Lloyd Dunn, a former President of the Council for Exceptional Children, attacked this provision on the grounds that it "does not move us toward the normalization and integration of services for children with learning problems but will have the reverse impact." Instead, he went on to say, it will create "special education domains at the expense of many other professionals equally competent and ready to serve children with school problems."[20]

By the mid-1980s Dunn's doubts about least restrictive placements had spurred on a full-scale oppositional movement known as the Regular Education Initiative, or simply REI. Like Dunn, proponents of REI argue that the least restrictive environment provision has not done away with segregated special education. Disabled children, they claim, remain as segregated as they were before the implementation of P.L. 92–142. REI supporters differ among themselves on how to reduce this isolation. Some call for increased cooperation between special and regular educators to enable more mildly handicapped and even some severely handicapped children to be placed in regular classrooms. Others recommend the virtual merging of regular, special, and compensatory education so that all children will receive instruction in regular classrooms. Most supporters of this movement take positions somewhere in-between.[21] Proponents of REI have certainly provoked those who support the practice of least restrictive placements. One such advocate depicted the REI as the educational equivalent of the so-called trickle-down economic practices of Presidents Reagan and Bush. Just as this economic strategy has been criticized for aiding the most prosperous at the expense of the poor, this critic claims that REI will aid those students who have little difficulty at the expense of those with the greatest problems.[22] It is not clear at this point what impact REI is having on school practice. Nevertheless, the very presence of this movement and the rancor it has engendered among educators does point to an uncertain future for segregated special education.

V.

A final sign of a growing dissatisfaction with prevailing views about educating children with learning problems is the continuing conceptual crisis facing the learning disabilities field. In the decade following the implementation of P.L. 94–142, the number of learning disabled children who were served in special education programs increased by 134 percent from

796 thousand to over 1.8 million. By 1980 learning disabled children became the largest group of exceptional students served in the public schools.[23] Despite this growth, the same doubts that have always existed about learning disabilities remain. The evidence for its neurological origins is just as elusive today as it was when Strauss and Werner first postulated the existence of the supposed brain-injured child.[24] Similarly, many contemporary researchers appear as skeptical as did Seymour Sarason in 1940 about the neurological roots of this condition.[25] As a consequence, the field's current experts seem preoccupied with trying to figure out precisely what a learning disability is. They certainly seem as divided as were their counterparts during the 1960s in settling on a definition of this condition.[26]

Between 1977 and 1982, the U.S. Department of Education funded research centers at five universities to investigate a variety of issues related to the education of learning disabled children and adolescents. In a special issue of *Exceptional Education Quarterly*, published in the Spring of 1983, representatives of the institutes—located at the Universities of Illinois at Chicago, Kansas, Minnesota, Virginia, and at Teachers College, Columbia University—offered assessments of their research efforts. Taken together, the five essays painted a positive picture, noting particular successes in identifying important characteristics of learning disabled children and in developing some apparently promising instructional techniques.[27]

In addition to the review essays, the journal published commentaries by two learning disabilities researchers who were not affiliated with the institutes. While these commentators were generally positive in their assessment of this body of research, they did point to certain problems. As Barbara Keogh saw it, the institutes did little to explain the actual nature of learning disabilities as a handicapping condition.[28] Similarly, James McKinney noted that despite their collective efforts, these institutes were not able to provide much guidance for differentiating learning disabled children from other low-achievers.[29] Notwithstanding his recognition of this weakness, McKinney singled out the Minnesota institute for criticism precisely because so much of its work highlighted this difficulty. He charged the Minnesota researchers with undermining public confidence in the viability of learning disabilities as a diagnostic category.[30] In a response to McKinney, a number of members of the Minnesota institute noted how vague the concept of learning disabilities was. Learning disabilities, as they put it, is "whatever society wants it to be, needs it to be, or will permit it to be."[31]

Despite the current size of the learning disabled student population, its rate of growth appears to be declining. Between 1977 and 1981, the percentage of learning disabled children served in public school special education programs increased about fifteen percent a year. Between 1981 and 1985, the percentage increased only about three and half percent a year. Some of this decline is undoubtedly due to the increasing success of the nation's public schools in identifying learning disabled children. Whereas about a quarter of children with learning disabilities were being accommodated in the nation's public schools before the enactment of P.L. 94–142, about eighty percent of these children were being served by the mid-1980s.[32] Yet this diminishing growth rate may also reflect persisting doubts about learning disabilities itself. With the development of a medicalized discourse for talking about low-achievement, learning disabilities came to supplant backwardness as a public school vehicle for accommodating low-achieving children. Likewise, continuing uncertainties about the soundness of learning disabilities as a diagnostic category may undermine its usefulness as an educational label.

Taken together, criticisms of curriculum differentiation, attacks on segregated special education, and the apparent conceptual inadequacies of the concept of learning disabilities point to the need for a reconceptualization of the problem of childhood learning difficulties. The emerging at-risk child movement may represent that new understanding.

VI.

The great promise of conceptualizing childhood learning difficulties as an at-risk problem is that by doing so we may be able to reconcile the contradictions that have impeded the efforts of twentieth-century school managers to accommodate difficult to teach students. Such initiatives as curriculum integration, accelerated schooling, and the establishment of school health clinics do not force school managers to choose between the interests of able students and those with learning difficulties. Rather, they are efforts that help low-achieving children by enriching the school experiences of all children.[33] It is, of course, not inevitable that school programs for at-risk children will evolve in this direction. School managers can, as we have seen, embrace the at-risk label and continue the practice of consigning such children to separate and segregated programs.

Proponents of the at-risk movement face a critical dilemma. The current pattern of organizing schools, Gary Natriello, Edward McDill, and Aaron Pallas argue, is based on two assumptions. American students, according to the first of these suppositions, are a relatively homogeneous group of individuals who exhibit, as they put it, "fairly uniform middle-class characteristics." In carrying on their work, they go on to say, schools seem to take for granted that their clientele can easily acquire or already possess essential reading, writing, and arithmetic skills; exhibit appropriate social behavior; and require a similar and predetermined educational experience. Second, the prevailing organization assumes that the essential task, and perhaps sole mission, of the nation's schools is to provide instruction in the traditional disciplines of knowledge. It is presumed whatever other needs that children have will be met by their families or the communities in which they live.[34]

The reality of public schooling, as we have seen throughout this book, belies these two assumptions. From the turn of this century onward, the nation's schools have struggled to accommodate an increasingly diverse array of students who differ in their backgrounds, abilities, interests, and inclinations. Children with learning difficulties—whether we label them backward, learning disabled, or at-risk—are a prime example of this diverse makeup. Many do not possess the requisite academic skills to be successful in schools. Those who have them, seem unable to utilize them. Such children often exhibit behavioral problems. And these are children who need more from the schools than academic instruction. They typically bring with them into the classroom a host of interpersonal problems and family and community conflicts that require psychological and social intervention.

The challenge facing those who champion the cause of at-risk children, again according to Natriello, McDill, and Pallas, is to develop organizational schemes that possess sufficient flexibility to provide for this heterogenenous population.[35] The temptation facing school managers, as we have seen throughout this book, is to defer any effort at a fundamental restructuring of schools that create the capacity for this flexibility. Instead they have embraced and continue to support a recalibrated and unauthentic common school ideal that relies on the addition of segregated programs for difficult to teach children. The at-risk movement represents a critical dividing point in this century-long effort of American school managers to accommodate children with learning difficulties. They can embrace those elements of this movement that, not unlike their efforts during the last eighty or so years, provide for difficult to teach children with separate and distinct educational programs. Or they can select the newer and conceptually richer route of this reform initiative toward a restructured school.

Even if school managers take on the difficult task of restructuring the schools to serve all children, there is no guarantee that they will be successful. The experience of the New Futures Initiative is illustrative of the difficulty such efforts encounter. One purpose of the Dayton and Little Rock middle school clustering plan, which I described earlier in this chapter, was to provide for curriculum integration. In Little Rock the most that teachers could accomplish was to organize more effectively the teaching of similar topics that were already a part of the existing curriculum. And in Dayton only a few teachers were willing to experiment with integration and their efforts usually involved units within courses, not the courses themselves.[36]

A second goal of these clusters was to allow teachers to meet and talk together to enhance their knowledge of their students. This goal was not, however, realized. The common planning provided in this plan became a forum where teachers discussed the problems of these children and their families and often recommended referring them to psychological counseling or other social services. Teachers in Dayton and Little Rock are, it seems, having as much difficulty in reorganizing their schools for at-risk children as were Minneapolis's teachers some forty years ago when that city adopted the B Curriculum Experiment.

*   *   *

As a historian, I have always tried to resist the allure of searching for specific contemporary lessons in our study of the past. Yet I do think that history offers us a lens for illuminating issues of educational policy. Our examination of the initiatives advanced by twentieth-century school managers for accommodating children with learning difficulties can enable us to look at the problem of at-risk children in new and interesting ways, and as a consequence to ask different questions than we presently do.

In this vein, our study of what I suggested at the beginning of this volume was the first attempt to educate at-risk children should lead us to ask a very different question than we have been asking up to now. We do not need to ask how public schools as they are presently arranged can accommodate low-achieving children. Asking such a question will only lead us along the path to a differentiated school program. Rather we need to ask how we can reorganize schools to enhance the quality of education for all children. It is only when we ask this question that we will be truly ready to accommodate children with learning difficulties in our schools.

From the first, the efforts of American school managers to provide for students with learning difficulties have pulled them in contradictory directions. Not certain as to whether they wanted to provide for the individual needs of these children or to assure the uninterrupted progress of the regular classroom, these educators embraced a recalibrated common school ideal that resolved their dilemma through curriculum differentiation. The result has been the creation of an array of special programs to remove these children from regular classrooms. Throughout this century we have viewed children with learning difficulties differently. Early in the century, we thought of them as being backward. By mid-century, we saw them as being learning disabled. Today, we label them as being at-risk. Our labels, it seems, have changed, but our reliance on segregation has persisted.

Although never completely realized, the ideal of common schooling first spelled out by mid-nineteenth-century school reformers provides a moral compass for our efforts to improve education.[37] Whether we are talking about inequities in school financing, unfair allocations of curricular and instructional resources, or racial and ethnic segregation—to name but a few—this ideal has directed us, often unwillingly, toward solutions that embody our most democratic and egalitarian impulses. If those impulses are to serve us today in addressing the needs of children with learning difficulties, we must go against the grain and reassert an authentic version of our common school ideal.

Notes

Chapter 1.

1. *Minneapolis Tribune*, February 2, 1974.

2. Ibid., February 17, 1974.

3. Not unlike the learning disabilities literature of the 1960s and 70s, research and writing on at-risk children appears to be the educational growth industry of the 1990s. For examples of this literature, see the following: Carnegie Council on Adolescent Development, *Turning Points: Preparing American Youth for the 21st Century* (Washington, D.C.: Carnegie Council on Adolescent Development, 1989); Wendy S. Hopfenberg and others, *Toward Accelerated Middle Schools for At-Risk Youth*, Report of the Project to Develop Accelerated Middle Schools for Disadvantaged Youth, Stanford University, February 1990; Henry M. Levin, "New Schools for the Disadvantaged," *Teacher Education Quarterly* 14 (Fall 1987), 60–83; National Commission on the Role of the School and the Community in Improving Adolescent Health, *Code Blue: Uniting for Healthier Youth* (Alexandria: National Association of State Boards of Education, 1990); Gary Natriello, ed., *School Dropouts: Patterns and Policies* (New York: Teachers College, 1987); Robert Slavin, Nancy L. Karweit, and Nancy A. Madden, eds. *Effective Programs for Students At Risk* (Boston: Allyn and Bacon, 1989); Gary Wehlage and others, *Reducing the Risk: Schools as Communities of Support* (New York: The Falmer Press, 1989).

4. Researchers have located the origins of contemporary efforts to educate at-risk children in a variety of times and places. Some trace these efforts as far back as the attempts of seventeenth-century colonial Americans to provide for dependent children. Others look to the campaign of early nineteenth-century reformers against childhood poverty. And still others link this contemporary reform initiative to the the late nineteenth-century child saving movement. See Hamilton Cravens, "Child Saving in Modern America, 1870s–1990s," in *Children At-Risk in America: History, Concepts, and Public Policy*, ed. Roberta Wollons (Albany: State University of New York Press, 1993), 3–31; Larry Cuban, "The 'At-Risk' Label and the Problem of Urban School Reform," *Phi Delta Kappan* 70 (June 1989), 780–84, 799–801; Elizabeth Blue Swadener, "Children and Families 'At Risk:' Etiology, Critique, and Alternative Paradigms," *Educational Foundations* 4 (Fall 1990), 17–39.

5. Emile Durkheim, *The Evolution of Educational Thought: Lectures on the Formation and Development of Secondary Education in France*, trans. Peter Collins (London: Routledge and Kegan Paul, 1979), 9.

6. Ibid., 126; Herbert M. Kliebard and Barry M. Franklin, "The Course of the Course of Study," in *Historical Inquiry in Education: A Research Agenda*, ed. John Hardin Best (Washington, D.C.: American Educational Research Association, 1983), 152–53.

7. James M. Kauffman and Patricia L. Pullen, "An Historical Perspective: A Personal Perspective on our History of Service to Mildly Handicapped and At-Risk Students," *Remedial and Special Education* 10 (November/December 1989), 12–14; Maynard C. Reynolds, "An Historical Perspective: The Delivery of Special Education to Mildly Disabled and At-Risk Students," *Remedial and Special Education* 10 (November/December 1989), 7–11; United States Department of Education, Information Services, Office of Educational Research and Improvement, *Increasing Achievement of At-Risk Students at Each Grade Level*, by James M. McPartland and Robert E. Slavin, Policy Perspective Series (Washington, D.C.: GPO, 1990), 4–6.

8. Slavin, Karweit, and Madden, *Effective Programs*, 5.

9. Wehlage and others, *Reducing the Risk*, 7–27, 48–74; Hopfenberg and others, *Middle Schools*, 1.

10. For a similar viewpoint, see Sally Lubeck and Patricia Gar-

rett, "The Social Construction of the 'At-risk' Child," *British Journal of Sociology of Education* 11, no. 3 (190), 327–40.

11. *Seventh Annual Report of the Lake View High School,* June 1881.

12. William J. Reese, *Power and the Promise of School Reform: Grass-roots Movements During the Progressive Era* (Boston: Routledge and Kegan Paul, 1986), 148–76, 209–37; Michael W. Sedlak and Robert L. Church, *A History of Social Services Directed to Youth,* Final Report, National Institute of Education, Contract no. 400–79–0017, 1982, 20–34; Michael W. Sedlak and Steven Schlossman, "The Public School and Social Services: Reassessing the Progressive Legacy," *Educational Theory* 35 (Fall 1985), 371–83; Theda Skocpol, *Protecting Soldiers and Mothers: The Political Origins of Social Policy in the United States* (Cambridge: Belknap Press of Harvard University, 1992), 45–47; David Tyack, "The High School as a Social Service Agency: Historical Perspectives on Current Policy Issues," *Educational Evaluation and Policy Analysis* 1 (September-October 1979), 54–57.

13. Rhoda Esten, "Backward Children in the Public Schools," *Journal of Psycho-Asthenics* 5 (September 1900), 11–12; David Mitchell, *Schools and Classes for Exceptional Children* (Cleveland: The Survey Committee of the Cleveland Foundation, 1916), 9; Department of Interior, *Public School Education of Atypical Children,* by Robert Kunzig, Bulletin, 1931, no. 10 (Washington, D.C.: GPO, 1931), 70.

14. E. Anne Bennison, "Creating Categories of Competence: The Education of Exceptional Children in the Milwaukee Public Schools, 1908–1917," Ph.D. diss., University of Wisconsin, Madison, 1988, 18–21; Barry M. Franklin, "Progressivism and Curriculum Differentiation: Special Classes in the Atlanta Public Schools, 1898–1923," *History of Education Quarterly* 29 (Winter 1989), 571–93; Irving G. Hendrick and Donald L. MacMillan, "Selecting Children for Special Education in New York City: William Maxwell, Elizabeth Farrell, and the Development of Ungraded Classes, 1900–1920," *Journal of Special Education* 22 (Winter 1989), 395–417; Marvin Lazerson, "The Origin of Special Education," in *Special Education Policies: Their History, Implementation, and Finance,* eds. Jay G. Chambers and William T. Hartman (Philadelphia: Temple University Press, 1983), 15–33; Seymour B. Sarason and John Doris, *Educational Handicap, Public Policy, and Social History: A Broad-*

ened Perspective on Mental Retardation (New York: Free Press, 1979), 262–68, 275–79.

15. Detroit Board of Education, *Fifty-Third Annual Report*, 1896, 163, Detroit Public School Archives (hereafter DEA).

16. New York City Board of Education, *Twentieth, Twenty-First and Twenty-Second Annual Report*, 1918–1920, 7, New York City Board of Education Archives, Milbank Memorial Library, Teachers College, Columbia University (hereafter NYC).

17. Atlanta Board of Education, *Minutes*, December 21, 1916, 7:3, Atlanta Public School Archives (hereafter APSA).

18. C.G. Pearse, "Schools for Defectives in Connection with the Public Schools," *Journal of Proceedings and Addresses of the Forty Fifth Annual Meeting of the National Education Association*, Los Angeles, California, July 8–12, 1907, 116. I am indebted to E. Anne Bennison for bringing this quote to my attention. See Bennison, "Creating," 154.

19. I have drawn my account of this transformation from the following sources: Michel Foucault, *Discipline and Punish: The Birth of the Prison*, trans. Alan Sheridan (New York: Vintage Books, 1977), 3–69, 73–131; idem, "Prison Talk," in *Power/Knowledge: Selected Interviews and Other Writings, 1972–1977*, ed. Colin Gordon, trans. Colin Gordon, Leo Marshall, John Mepham, and Kate Sopher (New York: Pantheon, 1980), 37–54; idem, "The Dangerous Individual," in *Politics, Philosophy, Culture: Interviews and Other Writings, 1977–1984*, ed. Lawrence D. Kritzman, trans. Alan Sheridan and others (New York: Routledge, 1988), 125–51; David Ingleby, "Mental Health and Social Order," in *Social Control and the State*, eds. Stanley Cohen and Andrew Scull (Oxford: Basil Blackwell, 1983), 141–88; Joan Busfield, *Managing Madness: Changing Ideas and Practice* (London: Unwin Hyman, 1986), 80–148.

20. David Rothman, *The Discovery of the Asylum: Social Order and Disorder in the New Republic* (Boston: Little, Brown, and Company, 1971), xiii–xx, 3–56, 79–205; William G. Staples, *Castles of Our Conscience: Social Control and the American State, 1800–1985* (New Brunswick: Rutgers University Press, 1990), 19–48.

21. Edward A. Ross, *Seventy Years of It* (New York: Appleton-Century, 1936), 54.

22. For an extended discussion of Ross's life and work, see Barry

M. Franklin, *Building the American Community: The School Curriculum and the Search for Social Control* (London: Falmer Press, 1986), 15–28.

23. William M. Kolb, "The Sociological Theories of Edward Alsworth Ross," in *An Introduction to the History of Sociology*, ed. Harry Elmer Barnes, abridged ed. (Chicago: University of Chicago Press, 1966), 458.

24. Franklin, *Building*, 28–37.

25. Barry M. Franklin, "Self Control and the Psychology of School Discipline," in *Contemporary Curriculum Discourse*, ed. William F. Pinar (Scottsdale: Gorsuch Scarisbrick, 1988), 35–36.

26. Emerson E. White, *School Management: A Practical Treatise for Teachers and All Other Persons Interested in the Right Training of the Young* (New York: American Book Company, 1893), 168.

27. R. L. Lyman, "The Washington Junior High School, Rochester, New York," *School Review* 28 (March 1920), 178–204.

28. Theresa R. Richardson, *The Century of the Child: The Mental Hygiene Movement and Social Policy in the United States and Canada* (Albany: State University of New York Press, 1989), 1–2, 45–57.

29. Ibid., 53–54.

30. Ibid., 87–90; Sol Cohen, "The Mental Hygiene Movement, the Commonwealth Fund, and Public Education, 1921–1933," in *Private Philanthropy and Public Elementary and Secondary Education.* Proceedings of the Rockefeller Archive Center Conference, June 8, 1979, ed. Gerald Benjamin (North Tarrytown: Rockefeller Archives Center, 1980), 34–46; Margo Horn, *Before It's Too Late: The Child Guidance Movement in the United States, 1922–1945* (Philadelphia: Temple University Press, 1989), 9–10, 30–31, 62–63.

31. I have drawn my account of the medicalization of deviance from the following sources: Busfield, *Managing Madness*, 116–21, 358–60; Staples, *Castles*, 138–45; Peter Conrad, "Medicalization and Social Control," *Annual Review of Sociology* 18 (1992), 209–32; Peter Conrad and Joseph W. Schneider, *Deviance and Medicalization: From Badness to Sickness*, expanded ed. (Philadelphia: Temple University Press, 1992), 32–35; Nicholas N. Kittrie, *The Right to be Different: Deviance and Enforced Therapy* (Baltimore: Johns Hopkins

University Press, 1971), 346–350; Charles Rosenberg, "Disease and Social Order in America: Perceptions and Expectations," in *AIDS: The Burden of History*, eds. Elizabeth Fee and Daniel M. Fox (Berkeley: University of California Press, 1988), 12–32; Irving Kenneth Zola, "Medicine as an Institution of Social Control," *The Sociological Review* 20 (November 1972), 487–504.

32. Conrad and Schneider, *Deviance*, 156–61, 284–85.

33. Sarason and Doris, *Educational Handicap*, 300–309; Leonard P. Ayres, *Laggards in Our Schools: A Study of Retardation and Elimination in City School Systems* (New York: Survey Associates, 1909), 1–7; Bureau of Education, *Provision for Exceptional Children in Public Schools*, by James H. Van Sickle, Lightner Witmer, and Leonard P. Ayres, Bulletin, 1911, no. 14 (Washington, D.C.: GPO, 1911), 17; Paul Hanus, "Introduction," in *School Training of Defective Children*, by Henry H. Goddard (New York: World Book Company, 1914), xvi–xvii; Barbara S. Morgan, *The Backward Child: A Study of the Psychology and Treatment of Backwardness* (New York: G.P. Putnam's Sons, 1914), 1–4.

34. Howard McQueary, "The Relation of the Public School and the Special School," in *Proceedings of the Seventh Annual Conference on the Education of Backward, Truant, Delinquent, and Dependent Children* (Westboro: The Lyman School for Boys, 1910), 122–23.

35. Hanus, "Introduction," xvi.

36. Florence McNeal, "Ungraded Schools for Backward Children as a Means for Reclaiming Delinquent Children," *Proceedings of the Sixth Annual Conference on the Education of Backward, Truant, and Delinquent Children* (Buffalo: Glen Mills School of Printing, 1909), 62–63.

37. William L. Bodine, "The Cause and the Cure," *Proceedings of the Second National Conference on the Education of Backward, Truant, and Delinquent Children* (Plainfield: Indiana Boys School, 1905), 64–67.

38. Ibid., 66.

39. Charles C. Krauskopf, "The Instruction of Backward Children," *Proceedings of Second National Conference. . .* , 85–94.

40. Ibid., 97.

41. Morgan, *Backward Child*, 21.

42. Annie D. Inskeep, *Teaching Dull and Retarded Children* (New York: Macmillan, 1926), 39.

43. Nelson McLain, "Elementary Instruction in Agriculture in Schools for Backward, Truant, and Delinquent Children," *Proceedings of the Second National Conference. . .* , 6–7.

44. William Shearer, "Why So Many Children are Backward and How the Number can be Reduced," *Proceedings of the Third National Conference on the Education of Backward, Truant, and Delinquent Children* (Lancaster: Boys Industrial School, 1906), 27.

45. Ibid., 30.

46. Ibid., 39.

47. Krauskopf, "Instruction," 89–90.

48. I have derived my definition of the state from the accounts of Martin Carnoy, Eric Nordlinger, Theda Skocpol, and Thomas Popkewitz. See Martin Carnoy, *The State and Political Theory* (Princeton: Princeton University Press, 1984), 3; Eric Nordlinger, *On the Autonomy of the Democratic State* (Cambridge: Harvard University Press, 1981), 11; Theda Skocpol, "Bringing the State Back In: Strategies of Analysis in Current Research," in *Bringing the State Back In*, eds. Peter B. Evans, Dietrich Rueschemeyer, and Theda Skocpol (Cambridge: Cambridge University Press, 1985, 3–37; Thomas S. Popkewitz, *A Political Sociology of Educational Reform: Power/Knowledge in Teaching, Teacher Education, and Research* (New York: Teachers College Press, 1991), 41–43. I am indebted to Joseph Tropea for first alerting me to the importance of the state in explaining the development of special education. For his use of the state in interpreting the history of special education, see Joseph Tropea, "Bureaucratic Order and Special Children: Urban Schools, 1890s–1940s," *History of Education Quarterly* 27 (Spring 1987), 29–53; and "Bureaucratic Order and Special Children: Urban Schools, 1950s–1960s," *History of Education Quarterly* 27 (Fall 1987), 339–61.

49. For an examination of this process of "state-building," see Stephen Skowronek, *Building a New American State: The Expansion of National Administrative Capacities, 1877–1920* (Cambridge: Cambridge University Press, 1982), vii–viii, 3–18, 210.

50. Ibid., 248–284.

51. Schools, according to Abram de Swaan, represent one element of the state apparatus of modern industrialized societies. In-

creasing enrollments, he believes, were the precipitating force behind the expansion of schooling, including the appearance of special education. "Having persuaded so many of the desirability of schooling, the schoolmen finally succeeded in making it indispensable for everyone; the emergence of illiteracy as a new category of deficiency, as a residue of ignorance, signified the final victory of literacy. Universal elementary education created residual problem categories of 'unteachables,' 'unreachables,' and 'school leavers' which in this century became the object of intervention by specialized pedagogic experts." See Abram deSwaan, *In Care of the State: Health Care, Education, and Welfare in Europe and the USA in the Modern Era* (New York: Oxford University Press, 1988), 234–35.

52. Lester M. Salamon, "Of Market Failure, Voluntary Failure, and Third Party Government: Toward a Theory of Government-Nonprofit Relations in the Modern Welfare State," in *Shifting the Debate: Public/Private Sector Relations in the Modern Welfare State*, eds. Susan A. Ostrander and Stuart Langton (New Brunswick: Transaction Books, 1987), 31–37.

53. I selected these two sites on the basis of the quality of their public school archives. In comparison to other cities that I visited, including Chicago, Detroit, and New York, these two schools systems had more extensive collections of documents dealing with the early history of special and remedial education. Atlanta and Minneapolis were particularly rich sources for the kinds of internal administrative reports and memoranda and student records needed to reconstruct the curriculum changes and classroom practices detailed in this volume. Needless to say, it is difficult to generalize about national developments from a study of only two cities. Yet my examination of the less extensive records available in Chicago, Detroit, and New York, along with my reading of a number of secondary studies (see footnotes 10 and 47), suggests that what occurred in both Atlanta and Minneapolis roughly parallels events in other urban school systems during this period.

Chapter 2.

1. The joint commitment to accessibility and a shared educational experience can be thought of as constituting the ideal of mid–nineteenth-century common school reform. For a discussion of this ideal, see Lawrence Cremin, *American Education: The National Ex-*

perience, 1783–1876 (New York: Harper and Row, 1980), 138, 156–157; Carl Kaestle, *Pillars of the Republic: Common Schools and American Society, 1780–1860* (New York: Hill and Wang, 1983), xi, 99–100, 116; Ira F. Katznelson and Margaret Weir, *Schooling for All: Class, Race, and the Decline of the Democratic Ideal* (New York: Basic Books, 1985), 54–57; David F. Labaree, *The Making of an American High School: The Credentials Market and the Central High School of Philadelphia, 1838–1939* (New Haven: Yale University Press, 1988), 12–27; David Tyack and Elisabeth Hansot, *Managers of Virtue: Public School Leadership in America, 1820–1980* (New York: Basic Books, 1982), 20–25; Maris A. Vinovskis, *The Origins of Public High Schools: A Reexamination of the Beverly High School Controversy* (Madison: University of Wisconsin Press, 1985), 19.

2. Charles F. Mercer, *A Discourse on Popular Education* (Princeton: Princeton Press, 1826), 76.

3. Joint Committee of the Two Houses of the Pennsylvania Legislature, "The Pennsylvania Legislature Advocates a General System of Common Schools," in *Education in the United States: A Documentary History*, ed. Sol Cohen (New York: Random House, 1974), 2:1002.

4. David Tyack and Elisabeth Hansot, *Learning Together: A History of Co-Education in American Public Schools* (New Haven: Yale University Press, 1990), 46–113.

5. David L. Angus, "Class Conflict and the Nineteenth Century Public High School of the Midwest, 1845–1900," *Curriculum Inquiry* 18 (Spring 1988), 7–31; Gerald T. Burns, "Tradition and Revolution in the American Secondary Curriculum: The Cambridge High School Case," *Journal of Curriculum Studies* 20, no. 2 (1988), 97–118.

6. Robert L. Osgood, "Origins of Special Education in Boston: Intermediate Schools and Ungraded Classes." Paper presented at the annual meeting of the American Educational Research Association, Chicago, Illinois, April 3–7, 1991.

7. My discussion of the market economy is drawn from David John Hogan, *Class and Reform: School and Society in Chicago, 1880–1930* (Philadelphia: University of Pennsylvania Press, 1985), x–xiv, 1–3, 46–50; Harvey Kantor, *Learning to Earn: School, Work, and Vocational Reform in California, 1880–1930* (Madison: University of Wisconsin Press, 1988), 4–11; Karl Polanyi, *The Great Transformation* (Boston: Basic Books, 1957), 57, 68–69, 154; and Sean Wilentz, *Chants Democratic: New York City and the Rise of the American*

Working Class, 1788–1850 (New York: Oxford University Press, 1984), 3–19. Wilentz provides the clearest overview of the beginnings of this transformation: "In the most advanced parts of Britain and Europe, the interposition of merchant capital and continued expansion of capitalist markets rendered this duality a contradiction: gradually, from the sixteenth century through the early nineteenth, merchant capitalists and master craftsmen restructured the social relations of production, transformed wage labor into a market commodity, and established the basis for new sets of class relations and conflicts. In America, colonial rule, slavery (and other forms of unfree labor), the weakness of mercantilist guilds, and an abundance of land created a different economic matrix; nevertheless, a similar process occurred at an accelerated rate beginning in the late eighteenth century in the New England countryside and the established northern seaboard cities. Along with the destruction of plantation slavery, this disruption of the American artisan system of labor ranks as one of the outstanding triumphs of nineteenth-century American capitalism, part of the recording of formal social relations to fit the bourgeois ideal of labor, market, and man" (p. 5).

8. National Center for Educational Statistics, *Digest of Educational Statistics, 1989* (Washington, D.C.: GPO, 1989), 45.

9. See Kantor, *Learning*, 142–147; W. Norton Grubb and Marvin Lazerson, "Education and the Labor Market: Recycling the Youth Problem," in *Work, Youth, and Schooling: Historical Perspectives on Vocationalism in American Education*, eds. Harvey Kantor and David B. Tyack (Stanford: Stanford University Press, 1982), 110–41; David Hogan, "Making It in America: Work, Education, and Social Structure," ibid., 142–79.

10. Kantor, *Learning*, 17–44; Herbert M. Kliebard, *The Struggle for the American Curriculum, 1893–1958* (Boston: Routledge and Kegan Paul, 1986), 123–52.

11. Richard Joseph Hopkins, "Patterns of Persistence and Occupational Mobility in a Southern City: Atlanta, 1870–1920," Ph.D. diss., Emory University, 1972, 12–13; Department of the Interior, *Ninth Census, 1870* (Washington, D.C.: GPO, 1872), 1:102; Department of the Interior, *Tenth Census, 1880* (Washington, D.C.: GPO, 1883), 1:123; Department of the Interior, *Eleventh Census* (Washington, D.C.: GPO, 1895), 1:92; Department of Commerce, *Fourteenth Census, 1920* (Washington, D.C.: GPO, 1921), 1:195.

12. Hopkins, "Patterns," 15–23.

13. Melvin W. Ecke, *From Ivy Street to Kennedy Center: Centennial History of the Atlanta Public School System* (Atlanta: Atlanta Board of Education, 1972), 1–19; Marcia E. Turner, "Black School Population in Atlanta, Georgia, 1869–1949," in *Southern Cities, Southern Schools: Public Education in the Urban South*, eds. David N. Plank and Rick Ginsberg (Westport: Greenwood, 1991), 180–82.

14. George D. Strayer and N.L. Engelhardt, *Report of the Survey of the Public School System of Atlanta, Georgia* (New York: Division of Field Studies, Teachers College, 1921–22), 1:7–8.

15. Darlene Rebecca Roth, "Matronage: Patterns in Women's Organizations, Atlanta, Georgia 1890–1940," Ph.D. diss., George Washington University, 1978, 98.

16. Strayer and Engelhardt, *Report*, 1:8–10.

17. Atlanta Board of Education, *Minutes*, January 6, 1898, 2:522, APSA.

18. Ibid., September 24, 1908, 4:273, APSA.

19. Ibid., November 21, 1908, 4:285, APSA; *Atlanta Constitution*, November 26, 1908.

20. Atlanta Board of Education, *Minutes*, January 26, 1911, 5:123, APSA.

21. Ibid., January 4, 1912, 5:286, APSA.

22. Ibid., June 27, 1912, 5:356; July 25, 1912, 5:361, APSA; *Atlanta Constitution*, June 28, 1912, September 27, 1912.

23. Atlanta Board of Education, *Minutes*, December 15, 1914, 6:246–47; June 8, 1915, 6:295, APSA.

24. Ibid., June 29, 1915, 6:317, APSA.

25. Ibid., July 30, 1915, 6:330, APSA.

26. Ibid., APSA; *Atlanta Constitution*, July 31, 1915; Atlanta Board of Education, *School Directory*, 1915–1919, 19, 39, APSA.

27. Atlanta Board of Education, *School Directory*, 1920–1930, APSA. The two special classes for black children that were in existence in 1920, one at Carrie Steele School and the other at Pittsburg Night Schools, were closed the following year and replaced by two classes at Storrs School. The next year, however, those classes were also closed. There were no other special classes for black children

until 1929. For a discussion of special education for blacks in Georgia, see Jane Vivian Mack Strong, "A Study of Education Facilities Available to Atypical Negro and White Children in Georgia," M. Ed. thesis, Atlanta University, 1949.

28. Atlanta Board of Education, *Minutes,* June 22, 1916, 7:43, APSA.

29. Ibid., January 24, 1918, 8:7, APSA; Ecke, *Ivy Street,* 113.

30. Atlanta Board of Education, *School Directory,* 1920–1921, 1921–1922, APSA.

31. Atlanta Board of Education, *School Directory,* 1923–1924, APSA; *Atlanta Constitution,* March 25, 1928.

32. Atlanta Board of Education, *Minutes,* June 10, 1924, 12:161, APSA.

33. Atlanta Constitution, March 25, 1928; Atlanta Board of Education, *School Directory,* 1923–1930, APSA; Atlanta Board of Education, *Special Report Concerning Negotiations Between the Conference Committee of the Board of Education and the Citizens Advisory Committee, 1927,* APSA.

34. Detroit Board of Education, *Fortieth Annual Report of the Board of Education,* 1882–1883, 77–78, DEA; Detroit Board of Education, *Journal of Proceedings of the Board of Education,* 1883–1884, 18, 48, 63, DEA.

36. Detroit Board of Education, *Fifty-Ninth Annual Report of the Board of Education,* 1902, 158; *Sixty-Eighth Annual Report of the Board of Education,* 1910–1911, 124, DEA.

37. Detroit Board of Education, *Sixty-Third Annual Report of the Board of Education,* 1905–1906, 93, DEA.

38. Detroit Board of Education, *Sixty-Fourth Annual Report of the Board of Education,* 1906–1907, 75, DEA.

39. Detroit Board of Education, *Journal of Proceedings of the Board of Education,* 1907–1908, 249, DEA.

40. Detroit Board of Education, *Sixty-Eighth Annual Report of the Board of Education,* 1910–1911, 186; *Sixty-Ninth Annual Report of the Board of Education,* 1911–1912, 77–79, DEA; Detroit Board of Education, *The Department of Special Education,* 1925, 9–18, DEA.

41. Sarason and Doris, *Educational Handicaps,* 297.

42. New York City Board of Education, *Fifth Annual Report of the City Superintendent of Schools*, 1903, 114–17, NYC.

43. Julia Richmond, "Special Classes and Special Schools for Delinquent and Backward Children," in *Proceedings of the National Conference of Charities and Corrections*, Minneapolis, June 12–19, 1907, 236–37.

44. Atlanta Board of Education, *Twenty-Seventh Annual Report of the Board of Education*, December 31, 1898, 52–53; *Twenty-Eighth Annual Report of the Board of Education*, December 31, 1899, 28, APSA.

45. Atlanta Board of Education, *Minutes*, May 4, 1899, 3:72; May 23, 1899, 3:80, APSA.

46. Atlanta Board of Education, *Twenty-Ninth Annual Report of the Board of Education*, 1900, 21; *Thirtieth Annual Report of the Board of Education*, 1903, 54, APSA.

47. Atlanta Board of Education, *The Functioning of the Atlanta Public Schools*, 1928, 9, APSA.

48. See Franklin, *Building the American Community*, 104–7; Hogan, *Class and Reform*, xx–xxv, 138–39, 228–35; Kliebard, *Struggle for the American Curriculum*, 102–13; Martin Carnoy and Henry M. Levin, *Schooling and Work in the Democratic State* (Stanford: Stanford University Press, 1985), 80–97; Edward A. Krug, *The Shaping of the American High School, 1880–1920* (Madison: University of Wisconsin Press, 1969), 318–322; David Tyack, *The One Best System: A History of American Urban Education* (Cambridge: Harvard University Press, 1974), 182–188.

49. Georgia. *Education: Compulsory School Attendance (No. 576), Acts and Resolutions of the General Assembly of the State of Georgia (1916)*, Part I, Title 5, 101–4.

50. *Public School Education of Atypical Children . . .*, 24.

51. Georgia. *Child Labor in Factories Regulated (No. 399), Acts and Resolutions of the General Assembly of the State of Georgia (1906)*, Part I, Title 7, 98–100; Georgia. *Regulation Employment of Child Labor (No. 426), Acts and Resolutions of the General Assembly of the State of Georgia (1914)*, Part I, Title 5, 88–92.

52. Kenneth Coleman and others, *A History of Georgia*, 2d ed. (Athens: University of Georgia Press, 1977), 306.

53. David N. Plank, "Educational Reform and Organizational Change: Atlanta in the Progressive Era," in *Southern Cities, Southern Schools*, 133–49; David N. Plank and Paul E. Peterson, "Does Urban Reform Imply Class Conflict? The Case of Atlanta's Schools," in *The Social History of American Education*, eds. B. Edward McClellan and William J. Reese (Urbana: University of Illinois Press, 1988), 217–18; Paul E. Peterson, *The Politics of School Reform, 1870–1940* (Chicago: University of Chicago Press, 1985), 86.

54. I examined on a daily basis the *Atlanta Independent*, Atlanta's principal black newspaper, between 1916 and 1925, and the *Journal of Labor*, the official newspaper of the Atlanta Federation of Trades, between 1914 and 1921, and found no mention in either paper of low-achieving children or special classes.

55. I found only one reference to special classes in the papers of the Atlanta Public School Teachers' Association. At the February 1920 meeting of the Association's Board of Directors, Gussie Brenner, Principal of Fair Street School, noted the need for a "centrally located" facility to provide for the city's handicapped children. See Atlanta Public School Teachers Association, "Directors' Meeting," February 1920, Folder 3, Box 2072, Atlanta Education Association Collection, Southern Labor Archives, Special Collections, Georgia State University.

56. Atlanta City Council, "Evidence and Proceedings before a Special Committee of Five, Appointed under a Resolution of City Council," June 12, 1918, 386–89, Office of the City Clerk, Atlanta, Georgia.

57. Ibid., 263, 316–17.

58. Wayne Urban, "Progressive Education in the Urban South: The Reform of the Atlanta Schools, 1914–1918," in *The Age of Urban Reform: New Perspectives on the Progressive Era*, eds. Michael H. Ebner and Eugene M. Tobin (Port Washington: Kennikat, 1977), 137–38; Wayne Urban, "Educational Reform in a New South City: Atlanta, 1890–1925," in *Education and the Rise of the New South*, eds. Ronald Goodenow and Arthur O. White (Boston: G.K. Hall and Company, 1981), 118–19.

59. Atlanta Board of Education, *Minutes*, January 4, 1912, 5:288, APSA.

60. Ibid., April 8, 1914, 6:147–48, APSA.

61. Ecke, *Ivy Street*, 14, 16–17, passim; *Atlanta Constitution*, October 15, 1914, February 7, 1915.

62. Ecke, *Ivy Street*, 452–53.

63. Atlanta Board of Education, *Minutes*, October 22, 1914, 6:228–29, APSA; *Atlanta Constitution*, October 23, 1914.

64. For a discussion of how school reformers saw curriculum differentiation as a means of reconciling the public school's historical democratic goals of accessibility with the demands of a market economy, see Labaree, *Making*, 7–8, 70–72, 161–62, 173–77.

65. One of the reasons why those who manage the state undertake new initiatives, according to Margaret Weir and Theda Skocpol, is to advance their own professional and political agendas. They state that "government officials (or aspiring politicians) are quite likely to take a new initiative, conceivably well ahead of social demands, if existing state capacities can be readily adapted or reworked to do things that will bring advantage to them in their struggles with competitive political forces." See Margaret Weir and Theda Skocpol, "State Structures and the Possibilities for 'Keynesian' Responses to the Great Depression in Sweden, Britain, and the United States," in Evans, Rueschemeyer, and Skocpol, *Bringing*, 115.

66. Tyack and Hansot, *Managers of Virtue*, 106–14; Raymond E. Callahan, *Education and the Cult of Efficiency: A Study of the Social Forces that Have Shaped the Administration of the Public Schools* (Chicago: University of Chicago Press, 1962), 179–220.

67. For a discussion of the symbolic role of educational policy in legitimizing the educational professions, see Herbert M. Kliebard, "Curriculum Policy as Symbolic Action: Connecting Education with the Workplace," in *Case Studies in Curriculum Administration History*, eds. Henning Haft and Stefan Hopmann (London: Falmer Press, 1990), 143–58.

68. Tyack, *One Best System*, 185–86.

69. Atlanta Board of Education, *Minutes*, January 1, 1912, 5:286; March 28, 1912, 5:309, APSA; *Atlanta Constitution*, January 1, 1912.

70. Martin Schiesl, *The Politics of Efficiency: Municipal Administration and Reform in America, 1880–1920* (Berkeley: University of California Press, 1977), 115–30.

71. *Atlanta Constitution*, February 27, 1914; Urban, "Progressive Education in the Urban South," 132–33; Charles Strickland, "Parrish, Celeste Susannah," in *Notable American Women*, eds. Edward T. Jones, Janet Wilson-Jones, and Paul Boyer (Cambridge: Harvard University Press, 1971), 3:18–20.

72. Celeste S. Parrish, *Survey of the Atlanta Public Schools* (n.p., 1914; repr., Atlanta, 1973), 22.

73. Ibid., 27.

74. *Atlanta Constitution*, February 25, 1915.

75. Ecke, *Ivy Street*, 107–9; *Atlanta Constitution*, June 6, 1915, June 29, 1915; *Atlanta Journal*, June 29, 1915; Dorothy Orr, *A History of Education in Georgia* (Chapel Hill: University of North Carolina, 1950), 387.

76. *Atlanta Constitution*, March 25, 1928.

77. Detroit Board of Education, *Course of Study for Special Classes*, 1926, 9, 82–84.

78. Ibid., 8.

79. San Francisco Public Schools, *Course of Study for Atypical Classes*, 1926, 16; Minneapolis Public Schools, *Course of Study in Special Education for Retarded Children*, 1932–1933.

80. Atlanta Board of Education, *Curriculum Suggestions for Ungraded Classes—Junior High Schools*, 1938, 32–33.

81. Ibid., 41–44.

82. Strayer and Engelhardt, *Report*, 2:117; PTA Association, "Lee Street Enrollment, 1921–1922, 1922–1923," Box 2, Lee Street School Collection, Atlanta Historical Society.

83. Atlanta Board of Education, *Minutes*, July 27, 1916, 7:59, APSA.

84. This information could, of course, have been recorded elsewhere, but Delcie Schrider, Manager of the Atlanta Public Schools Record Center, was unaware of the existence of any other records for these children.

85. To protect the identity of the Lee Street special class students, I have given them pseudonyms that indicate their gender. For

a discussion of the meaning of the scores on this first version of the Stanford-Binet Test, see Lewis M. Terman, *The Measurement of Intelligence: An Explanation of and a Complete Guide for the Use of the Stanford Revision and Extension of the Binet-Simon Intelligence Scale* (Boston: Houghton Mifflin, 1916), 79–80.

86. In 1914 the Atlanta Board of Education adopted the following grading system: A (excellent), 90–100; B (good), 80–89; C (satisfactory), 70–79; D (fair), 60–69; E (unsatisfactory), below 60. In 1918 the Board introduced a new grading system: A (excellent), 90–100; B (good), 80–89; C (fair), 70–79; D (unsatisfactory), below 70. See Ecke, *Ivy Street*, 101, 129.

87. *Public School Education of Atypical Children*, 61–63.

88. White House Conference on Child Health and Protection, *The Handicapped Child: Report of the Committee on Physically and Mentally Handicapped* (New York: Century Company, 1933), 336.

Chapter 3.

1. Francis N. Maxfield, "Serious Mental Defect Without Feeblemindedness," *Ungraded* 11 (February 1926), 97–107.

2. Harry J. Baker, "The Diagnosis and Treatment of Maladjusted Children in the Detroit Public Schools," in *Preventing Crime: A Symposium*, eds. Sheldon Glueck and Eleanor Glueck (New York: McGraw-Hill, 1936), 160–61.

3. Alfred A. Strauss, "Typology in Mental Deficiency: Its Clinical, Psychological, and Educational Implications," *Journal of Psycho-Asthenics* 44 (June 1939), 85–90.

4. William M. Cruickshank and Daniel P. Hallahan, "Alfred A. Strauss: Pioneer in Learning Disabilities," in *Concepts in Special Education: Selected Writings*, ed. William M. Cruickshank (Syracuse: Syracuse University Press, 1981), 1:268–69.

5. Henry Head, *Aphasia and Kindred Disorders of Speech* (Cambridge: Cambridge University Press, 1926), 1:146, 221.

6. Kurt Goldstein, *The Organism* (New York: American Book Company, 1939), 31–61; Kurt Goldstein and D. Denny-Brown, *After*

Effects of Brain Injuries in War (New York: Grune and Stratton, 1942), 69–91.

7. Alfred Strauss and Heinz Werner, "Disorders of Conceptual Thinking in the Brain-Injured Child," Journal of Nervous and Mental Diseases 96 (August 1942), 168–72; Alfred Strauss and Laura Lehtinen, Psychopathology and Education of the Brain Injured Child (New York: Grune and Stratton, 1947), 1:13–15, 23–27.

8. Goldstein, The Organism, 17.

9. Alfred Strauss and Heinz Werner, "Comparative Psychopathology of the Brain-Injured Child and the Traumatic Brain-Injured Adult," American Journal of Psychology 99 (May 1943), 837.

10. Heinz Werner and Alfred Strauss, "Types of Visuo-Motor Activity in Their Relation to Low and High Performance Ages," Journal of Psycho-Asthenics 44 (June, 1939), 163–168.

11. Alfred Strauss and Heinz Werner, "Experimental Analysis of the Clinical Symptom 'Perseveration' in Mentally Retarded Children," American Journal of Mental Deficiency 47 (October 1942), 185–88.

12. Heinz Werner and Doris Carrison, "Animistic Thinking in Brain-Injured Mentally Retarded Children," Journal of Abnormal and Social Psychology 39 (January 1944), 43–62.

13. Heinz Werner and Alfred Strauss, "Pathology of Figure-Background Relation in the Child," Journal of Abnormal and Social Psychology 36 (April 1941), 236–48.

14. Alfred Strauss and Heinz Werner, "Disorders in Conceptual Thinking in the Brain-Injured Child," Journal of Nervous and Mental Diseases 96 (August 1942), 153–72.

15. Alfred Strauss and Heinz Werner, "The Mental Organization of the Brain-Injured Mentally Defective Child," American Journal of Psychiatry 97 (March 1941), 1202–3.

16. Strauss and Lehtinen, Psychopathology, 112.

17. Seymour Sarason, Psychological Problems in Mental Deficiency (New York: Harper and Row, 1949), 52–58.

18. Ibid., 58.

19. Goldstein, Organism, 18.

20. Ibid., 18–19.

21. Kurt Goldstein, *Language and Language Disturbances* (New York: Grune and Stratton, 1948), 1.

22. Strauss and Lehtinen, *Psychopathology*, 77.

23. Ibid.

24. Ibid., 112.

25. Ibid., 17.

26. Cruickshank, *Concepts* 1:266, 281–326.

27. Alfred Strauss and Newell Kephart, *Psychopathology and Education of the Brain-Injured Child* (New York: Grune and Stratton, 1955), 2:2.

28. Ibid., Appendix 2.

29. Gerald Coles, *The Learning Mystique: A Critical Look at "Learning Disabilities"* (New York: Pantheon Books, 1987), 3–7; J. Lee Wiederholt, "Historical Perspective on the Education of the Learning Disabled," in *The Second Review of Special Education*, eds. Lester Mann and David A. Sabatino (Philadelphia: JSE Press, 1974), 115–18.

30. Samuel T. Orton, *Reading, Writing and Speech Problems in Children* (New York: Norton, 1937), 11, 157; idem, "The 'Sight Reading' Method of Teaching Reading as a Source of Reading Disability," *Journal of Educational Psychology* 20 (1929), 141–42.

31. Orton, *Reading, Writing*, 48–53, 68, 126–28; idem, "Specific Reading Disability-Strephosymbolia," *Journal of the American Medical Association* 90 (1928), 1095–99.

32. Ibid., 69–98.

33. Ibid., 152–53.

34. Samuel T. Orton, "A Neurological Explanation of the Reading Disability," *Educational Record* 20 (January 1939), Supplement 12, 58–68; idem, "An Impediment to Learning to Read—A Neurological Explanation of the Reading Disability," *School and Society* 28 (September 8, 1928), 286–90.

35. The best treatment of the relationship between our discourse and our basic understanding of human beings is provided by Michel Foucault. See, for example, Michel Foucault, *The Birth of the Clinic: An Archaeology of Medical Perception*, trans. A. M. Sheridan Smith (New York: Vintage Books, 1973), x–xii, 196; and Hubert L.

Dreyfus and Paul Rabinow, *Michel Foucault: Beyond Structuralism and Hermeneutics*, 2d ed. (Chicago: University of Chicago Press, 1983), 14–16.

36. Conrad and Schneider, *Deviance*, 266–67.

37. Ibid., 267–68.

38. Fund for Perceptually Handicapped Children, *Proceedings of the Conference on Exploration into the Problems of the Perceptually Handicapped Child, April 6, 1963* (Evanston: Fund for Perceptually Handicapped Children, 1963), 42.

39. Ibid., 40–41; Donna Slettehaugh, interview by author, June 13, 1990, Minneapolis.

40. Fund for Perceptually Handicapped Children, *Proceedings*, 38–39.

41. Ibid., 38–64.

42. Samuel Kirk, "Introspection and Prophecy," in *Perspectives in Special Education: Personal Orientations*, eds. Burton Blatt and Richard J. Manis (Glenview: Scott, Foresman, 1984),28–31.

43. Samuel Kirk, "Behavioral Diagnosis and Remediation of Learning Disabilities," in Fund for Perceptually Handicapped Children, *Proceedings*, 1–3.

44. Robert Russell, "History of A.C.L.D.," March, 1973, Association for Learning Disabilities, Pittsburgh.

45. Department of Health, Education, and Welfare, *Task Force I—Minimal Brain Dysfunction in Children*, by Sam Clements, Public Health Service Publication no. 1415–1966 (Washington, D.C.: Department of Health, Education, and Welfare, 1966), 7–8.

46. William Cruickshank, *The Brain-Injured Child in Home, School, and Community* (Syracuse: Syracuse University Press, 1967), 27–55.

47. Newell Kephart, *The Slow Learner in the Classroom* (Columbus: Charles E. Merrill, 1960), 64–65.

48. Newell Kephart, *Learning Disability: An Educational Adventure* (West Lafayette: Kappa Delta Pi Press, 1968), 19–32.

49. Ibid., 27.

50. Ibid., 11–14.

51. Samuel A. Kirk and Winifred D. Kirk, *Psycholinguistic Learning Disabilities: Diagnosis and Remediation* (Urbana: University of Illinois Press, 1971), 3–13, 20–23.

52. National Advisory Committee on Handicapped Children, *Special Education for Handicapped Children: First National Report* (Washington, D.C.: U.S. Department of Health, Education, and Welfare, 1968), 34.

53. James C. Chalfant, *Identifying Learning Disabled Students: Guidelines for Decision Making* (Burlington: Northeast Regional Resource Center, 1984), 5, 132.

54. Patricia I. Myers and Donald D. Hammill, *Methods for Learning Disorders*, 2d ed. (New York: John Wiley and Sons, 1976), 8–10.

55. National Institute of Neurological Diseases and Stroke, *Central Processing Dysfunctions in Children: A Review of Research*, by James C. Chalfant and Margaret A. Scheffilin, NINDS Monograph no. 9 (Bethesda: U.S. Department of Health, Education, and Welfare, 1969), 147–48.

56. Ibid., 136.

57. Ibid., 137.

58. James Carrier, *Learning Disability: Social Class and the Construction of Inequality in American Education* (Westport: Greenwood Press, 1986), 93–104; Christine Sleeter, "Why Is There Learning Disabilities? A Critical Analysis of the Birth of the Field in Its Social Context," in *The Formation of the School Subjects: The Struggle for Creating an American Institution*, ed. Thomas S. Popkewitz (New York: Falmer Press, 1987), 224–32.

59. Ed N. Argulewicz, "Effects of Ethnic Membership, Socioeconomic Status, and Home Language on LD, EMR, and EH Placements," *Learning Disabilities Quarterly* 6 (Spring 1983), 195–200; Fay L. Brosnan, "Overrepresentation of Low Socioeconomic Minority Students in Special Education Programs in California," *Learning Disabilities Quarterly* 6 (Fall 1983), 517–25; James A. Tucker, "Ethnic Proportions in Classes for the Learning Disabled: Issues in Non Biased Assessment," *Journal of Special Education* 14 (Spring 1980), 93–105; Pamela Wright and Rafaela Santa Cruz, "Ethnic Composition of Special Education Programs in California," *Learning Disabilities Quarterly* 6 (Fall 1983), 387–94.

60. Kenneth T. Jackson, *Crabgrass Frontier: The Suburbanization of the United States* (New York: Oxford University Press, 1985), 232–38.

61. Coles, *Learning Mystique*, 141–49, 189–96.

62. Joan F. Goodman, "Organicity as a Construct in Psychological Diagnosis," in *Advances in School Psychology*, ed. Theodore R. Kratochwill (Hillsdale: Lawrence Erlbaum, 1983), 3:101–39.

63. Carol A. O'Connor, "Sorting Out the Suburbs: Patterns of Land Use, Class, and Culture," *American Quarterly* 37 (Special Issue, 1985), 382–84; Margaret Marsh, *Suburban Lives* (New Brunswick: Rutgers University Press, 1990), 182–89; Paul H. Mattingly, "Excavating the Historical Suburb," *American Quarterly* 41 (December 1989), 689–94; John R. Stilgoe, *Borderland: Origins of the American Suburb, 1820–1939* (New Haven: Yale University Press, 1988), 2–4.

64. Conrad and Schneider, *Deviance*, 269–71; Carrier, *Learning Disability*, 112; Congress, House, General Subcommittee on Education, *Hearings before the General Subcommittee on Education of the Committee on Education and Labor on H.R. 8660 and H.R. 9065, A Bill to Provide for Special Programs for Children with Learning Disabilities*, 91st Cong., 1st Sess., January 8, 9, and 10, 1969, 4–6.

65. Congress, *Hearings*, 160.

66. Ibid., 162–63.

67. Ibid., 54.

68. Ibid., 23.

69. Ibid., 56.

70. Ibid., 187.

71. Ibid., 192.

Chapter 4.

1. Atlanta Board of Education, *Minutes*, April 8, 1966, 71:3, 40, APSA.

2. Ibid., 41–42, APSA.

3. *Atlanta Journal*, October 1, 1916.

4. I have drawn my account of women's voluntarism from the following sources: Karen J. Blair, *The Clubwoman as Feminist: True Womanhood Redefined, 1868–1914* (New York: Holmes and Meier, 1980), 7–38, 93–119; Nancy F. Cott, *The Grounding of Modern Feminism* (New York: Yale University Press, 1987), 13–50; Sara Evans, *Born for Liberty: A History of Women in America* (New York: Free Press, 1989), 67–81, 138–52; Lori D. Ginzberg, *Women and the Work of Benevolence: Morality, Politics, and Class in the Nineteenth Century United States* (New Haven: Yale University Press, 1990), 36–66, 174–213; Theodora Penny Martin, *The Sound of Our Own Voices: Women's Study Clubs, 1860–1910* (Boston: Beacon Press, 1987), 14–47; Robin Muncy, *Creating a Female Dominion in American Reform, 1890–1935* (New York: Oxford University Press, 1991), 121–61; William L. O'Neill, *Everyone was Brave: The Rise and Fall of Feminism in America* (Chicago: Quadrangle Books, 1969), 77–106; Darlene Rebecca Roth, "Matronage: Patterns in Women's Organizations, Atlanta, Georgia 1890–1940," Ph.D. diss., George Washington University, 1978; Anne Firor Scott, *Making the Invisible Women Visible* (Urbana: University of Illinois Press, 1984), 259–94; idem, "On Seeing and Not Seeing: A Case of Historical Invisibility," *Journal of American History* 71 (June 1984), 7–21; idem, *Natural Allies: Women's Associations in American History* (Urbana: University of Illinois Press, 1991); Marsha Wedell, *Elite Women and the Reform Impulse in Memphis, 1875–1915* (Knoxville: University of Tennessee Press, 1991), 77–107.

5. Struthers Burt, "Junior League Ladies," *The Forum* 99 (June 1938), 327.

6. Ibid., 325.

7. Cleveland Amory, "The Junior League Gets Tough," *Saturday Evening Post*, February 7, 1948, 33.

8. Although the chapter was organized by members of the City's Debutante Clubs of 1915, 1916, and 1917, membership was not restricted to debutantes. Membership was open to any "girl" under the age of thirty who had resided in Atlanta or its suburbs for six months. Nonetheless, the nomination procedures for membership virtually ensured that new members were well known to current members and that they probably came from similar privileged backgrounds. Prospective members were proposed by two current members who wrote nomination letters to the Chair of the Membership Committee. If a prospective member was not known to the Committee, those sponsoring the nominee would have to secure three additional letters of

recommendation. When the necessary number of letters of recommendation were received, the nomination would be presented to the Board of Directors. The Board would elect the nominee providing she did not receive more than three negative votes. See *Annual Report of the Junior League*, 1920–1921, 25, Atlanta Junior League Collection, Atlanta Historical Society, Box 26, Folder 1 (hereafter AJLC). For a description of the elite background of League members, see Cheryl Lynn Dolinger, "Fine Ladies and Fine Motives: The Efforts of the Junior League in Child Welfare, 1930–1950," Senior Honors Paper, University of Minnesota, College of Liberal Arts, 1973, 3–4.

9. Irene Croft, "A Look into the Past of the Atlanta Junior League," *The Northside Neighbor*, October 31, 1968; Nell Felix Kirkland, "Well Dearie . . . Being a History of the Junior League of Atlanta, Along with Sundry and Sometime Nostalgic Guideposts Through Atlanta and the Nation from 1916 to the Present," 1959, AJLC, Box 2, Folder 4; Margaret E. Langford, "The Junior League of Atlanta: Celebrating 75 Years of Service," *Atlanta History* 35 (Fall 1991), 5.

10. Croft, "Junior League;" Langford, "A Look," 6.

11. *Annual Report of the Junior League of Atlanta*, 1920–1921, 12, AJLC; *Minutes of the Junior League of Atlanta*, November 1, 1919; December 3, 1919; February 3, 1920; January 4, 1921, AJLC, Box 22, Folder 1.

12. *Annual Report of the Junior League of Atlanta*, 1920–1921, 10, AJLC.

13. *Annual Report of the Junior League of Atlanta*, 1921–1922, 13, AJLC, Box 26, Folder 1.

14. Croft, "A Look."

15. *Annual Report of the Junior League of Atlanta*, 1920–1921, 5–7, AJLC.

16. *Minutes of the Junior League of Atlanta*, March 11, 1921; October 4, 1921; October 20, 1921, AJLC, Box 22, Folder 1; *Annual Report of the Junior League of Atlanta*, 1921–1922, 11, AJLC.

17. *Annual Report of the Junior League of Atlanta*, ibid., 5–6, AJLC.

18. *Annual Report of the Junior League of Atlanta*, 1922–1923, 5, AJLC, Box 26, Folder 1.

19. *Annual Report of the Junior League of Atlanta*, 1921–1922, 16, AJLC.

20. *Annual Report of the Junior League of Atlanta*, 1922–1923, 23; 1926–1927, 24, AJLC, Box 26, Folder 2.

21. *Annual Report of the Junior League of Atlanta*, 1927–1928, 1, AJLC, Box 26, Folder 2.

22. *Atlanta Constitution*, December 14, 1937.

23. *Annual Report of the Junior League of Atlanta*, 1936–1937, 1, AJLC, Box 26, Folder 4.

24. Katherine Hamm, "Personnel, Professionals, and Volunteers to Meet the Need," paper presented at the Fourteenth Annual Conference of the American Hearing Society, Chicago, June 9–12, 1959, 3, Atlanta Speech School Collection, Atlanta Historical Society, Box 1, Folder 8 (hereafter ASSC); "Biographical Note on Catherine Cathcart Hamm," ASSC, Box 1, Folder 9; "Atlanta's First Lady," *Junior League Magazine*, March 1947, ASSC, Box 1, Folder 5; *Charleston Evening Post*, January 25, 1945.

25. "Atlanta's First Lady," ASSC; *Minutes of the Junior League of Atlanta*, April 6, 1936, AJLC, Box 22, Folder 3; Anne Lindol, "Pioneer in Speech Correction," *The Wesleyan Alumnae*, 22 (February 1946), 1–2.

26. Atlanta Board of Education, *Minutes*, July 25, 1912, 5:361, APSA; Atlanta Board of Education, *Annual Report of the Superintendent of Schools*, 1937–1938, 111, APSA.

27. "A handwritten report submitted by Katherine C. Hamm on what is provided to speech handicapped children in Atlanta," September 22, 1937, 1–10, ASSC, Box 1, Folder 1.

28. "A handwritten report," ASSC; *Minutes of the Junior League of Atlanta*, May 28, 1937; March 1, 1938; March 29, 1938; April 1, 1938, Box 22, Folder 3, AJLC.

29. Katherine Cathcart Hamm, "Junior League School of Speech Correction," 1938, 2, ASSC, Box 1, Folder 12.

30. "A handwritten report," ASSC.

31. Ibid., ASSC; *Minutes of the Junior League of Atlanta*, May 27, 1938; May 31, 1938, AJLC, Box 22, Folder 3."

32. "Junior League School," 2, ASSC; *Atlanta Journal*, June 6, 1938.

33. "Junior League School," 2–3, ASSC; *Annual Report of the Junior League of Atlanta*, 1938–1939, 36–37, AJLC, Box 26, Folder 5; 1949–1950, 21–22; 1951–1952, 18–20; 1952–1953, 8, AJLC, Box 26, Folder 7.

34. Costello to Wills, February 5, 1947, ASSC, Box 1, Folder 10.

35. *Atlanta Constitution*, December 14, 1939; December 15, 1939; *New York Times*, December 15, 1939.

36. *Atlanta Constitution*, December 15, 1939; *Atlanta Daily World*, December 15, 1939.

37. *Atlanta Daily World*, December 20, 1939.

38. Langford, "Junior League," 11; *Minutes of the Junior League of Atlanta*, February 9, 1940; March 8, 1940, AJLC, Box 22, Folder 4; *Atlanta Constitution*, December 15, 1939.

39. *Atlanta Constitution*, December 14, 1939; December 15, 1939.

40. *Atlanta Journal*, December 14, 1939.

41. "A Brief History of the Junior League School for Speech Correction, 1938–1960," 3, ASSC, Box 1, Folder 1; Young to Hamm, September 26, 1947, ASSC, Box 1, Folder 10; Healey to Hamm, January 20, 1949, ASSC, Box 1, Folder 9; *Annual Report of the Junior League of Atlanta*, 1948–1949, 18–19, AJLC.

42. Dingman to Hoy, May 26, 1942, Association of Junior Leagues of America Collection, Social Welfare History Archives, University of Minnesota–Twin Cities (hereafter JLA), Box 4, Folder 36.

43. Huquinin to Van Shyok, undated (probably November or December 1944), JLA, Box 4, Folder 36.

44. Hamm, "Untitled Speech to the Annual Conference on Services to Handicapped Children in Florida," March 19–20, 1951, 9, ASSC, Box 1, Folder 8; *Annual Report of the Junior League of Atlanta*, 1949–1950, 21–22, AJLC, Box 26, Folder 6; 1950–1951, 12, AJLC, Box 26, Folder 7; *Minutes of the Junior League of Atlanta*, September 29, 1950, AJLC, Box 23, Folder 2; *Atlanta Journal*, September 14, 1950.

45. *Atlanta Journal*, June 6, 1938.

46. Strother to Dorsey, July 19, 1946, ASSC, Box 1, Folder 11.

47. Burke to Hamm, May 25, 1948, ASSC, Box 1, Folder 10.

48. *Minutes of the Junior League of Atlanta*, June 1954, AJLC, Box 23, Folder 2.

49. "A Brief History of the Junior League School," 7–9, ASSC.

50. Davidson to Junior League Speech School, June 27, 1946; June 28, 1946, ASSC, Box 1, Folder 11.

51. Drane to Hamm, August 5, 1946; August 8, 1946, ASSC, Box 1, Folder 11.

52. "A Brief History of the Junior League School," 8, ASSC.

53. Francis Ross, interview by author, March 1, 1989, Atlanta.

54. Advertisement that appeared in the 1954 Atlanta Opera program, ASSC, Box 1, Folder 5.

55. Tommie Parker, interview by author, March 2, 1989, Atlanta.

56. *The Voice*, September, 1963, ASSC, Box 1, Folder 2.

57. We should not, however, assume too much by the apparent similarity between the emerging discourse about learning disabilities and the practices of the Speech School. As David Tyack has perceptively warned us, there is no necessary one-to-one correspondence between what he calls "policy talk" and school practice. There are instances, and perhaps this is one, where the discourse that policy researchers use to frame their recommendations fits nicely with institutional practice. But there are many more cases in which this is not so. See David Tyack, "Public School Reform: Policy Talk and Institutional Practice," *American Journal of Education* 100 (November 1991), 1–19.

58. Katherine Hamm, "Untitled Speech to the Annual Conference on Services to Handicapped Children in Florida," March 19–20, 1951, 1, ASSC, Box 1, Folder 8.

59. Katherine Hamm, "Untitled Speech to the Junior League of Knoxville, Tennessee," May 1, 1956, 1–2, ASSC, Box 1, Folder 8.

60. Witherspoon to Richardson, October 15, 1937; December 29, 1937, JLA, Box 4, Folder 34.

61. Cox to Howlett, March 10, 1938, JLA, Box 4, Folder 34.

62. Howlett to Lucas, March 28, 1938, JLA, Box 4, Folder 34.

63. Lipscomb to Counts, November 28, 1940, JLA, Box 4, Folder 35; "Report of Field Visit made to Atlanta, Georgia, October 28– November 6, 1940," June 3, 1941, JLA, Box 4, Folder 35.

64. Van Sickler to Lipscomb, January 7, 1941; January 19, 1941, JLA, Box 4, Folder 35; "Report of a Field Visit to Atlanta, Georgia, October 31–November 5, 1944," n.d., JLA, Box 4, Folder 36.

65. Lipscomb to Taylor, November 19, 1940, JLA, Box 4, Folder 35; "Report of Field Visit to Atlanta, Georgia, October 28–November 6, 1940," JLA.

66. Van Sickler to Huquinin, November 24, 1946, JLA, Box 4, Folder 36.

67. *Minutes of the Junior League of Atlanta*, November 6, 1944, AJLC, Box 26, Folder 4; Atlanta Board of Education, *Making Americans: Superintendent's Annual Report*, 1943–1944, 10, APSA; Ecke, *Ivy Street*, 278.

68. Georgia Department of Education, *Sixty-Sixth and Sixty-Seventh Annual Report of the State Department of Education to the Georgia General Assembly*, June 20, 1938, 84; Georgia. *Equalizing Opportunities (No. 33), Acts and Resolutions of the General Assembly of the State of Georgia (1937)*, Part I—Title VII, 882–92.

69. *Atlanta Constitution*, September 5, 1945; Georgia. *Courses for Defective Speech and Hearing (no. 338), Acts and Resolutions of the General Assembly of the State of Georgia (1945)*, Part I—Title II, 312–15; Ellis Arnall, interview by author, September 29, 1989, Atlanta.

70. Text of an article for *Cotton Blossom*, October 1947, JLA, Box 4, Folder 39; *Annual Report of the Junior League of Atlanta*, 1945–1946, 6–7, AJLC, Box 29, Folder 1; Ecke, *Ivy Street*, 284, 296.

71. McCarty to Executive Board, February 9, 1948, 5, JLA, Box 4, Folder 40.

72. Ecke, *Ivy Street*, 308.

73. "Pertinent Facts on the Operation of the Atlanta Speech School Not Covered Completely in a Pamphlet Entitled *The Junior*

League's Speech School, Yesterday, Today, Tomorrow," 1946, JLA, Box 4, Folder 38.

74. McCarty to Burton, June 18, 1953, JLA, Box 5, Folder 44.

75. "Notes for Speech School Conference," 1950, 13, JLA, Box 5, Folder 42.

76. Georgia. *Education-Minimum Foundations Program (No. 333), Acts and Resolutions of the State of Georgia, 1949,* 1406–22.

77. "Notes for Speech School Conference," 8–9, JLA.

78. Atlanta Board of Education, Minutes, 57 (October 9, 1961), 2, APSA.

79. Georgia. *Minimum Foundation Program of Education Act (No. 523), Acts and Resolutions of the General Assembly of the State of Georgia, 1964,* General Acts and Resolutions, vol. 1, 19.

80. Ecke, *Ivy Street,* 402; *Minutes of the Junior League of Atlanta,* April 1967, AJLC, Box 24, Folder 4; *Annual Report of the Junior League of Atlanta,* 1966–1967, 16, AJLC, Box 30, Folder 4.

81. *Annual Report of the Junior League of Atlanta,* 1967–1968, 19, AJLC, Box 30, Folder 4; 1969–1970, 32, AJLC, Box 30, Folder 5; 1970–1971, 43–44, 60, AJLC, Box 30, Folder 5; *Atlanta Constitution,* March 10, 1969.

82. Georgia. *Education of Exceptional Children (No. 670), Acts and Resolutions of the General Assembly of the State of Georgia, 1968,* General Acts and Resolutions, vol. 1, 120–24.

83. *Minutes of the Junior League of Atlanta,* March 18, 1957; March 22, 1957, AJLC, Box 23, Folder 4; June 29, 1960, AJLC, Box 24, Folder 1.

84. Beth Stevens, "Blurring the Boundaries: How the Federal Government has Influenced Welfare Benefits in the Private Sector," in *The Politics of Social Policy in the United States,* eds. Margaret Weir, Ann Shola Orloff, and Theda Skocpol (Princeton: Princeton University Press, 1988), 147.

85. Today we would no doubt view the failure of the Speech School to accommodate black children as undermining the principle of common schooling. During the period we are considering, however, most Junior Leaguers probably took segregated schooling for granted. The existence of a racially segregated school system, to their

way of thinking, was not incompatible with support for the common school ideal.

Chapter 5.

1. Department of Commerce, *Twelfth Census, 1900* (Washington, D.C.: GPO, 1901), 624; Lucile M. Kane, *The Falls of St. Anthony: The Waterfall that Built Minneapolis* (St. Paul: Minnesota Historical Society, 1987), 30–41, 98–113; E. Dudley Parsons, *Making Minneapolis* (Minneapolis, 1926), 51–53, 60–62.

2. Department of Commerce, *Fifteenth Census, 1930*, vol. 3, part 1 (Washington, D.C.: GPO, 1932), 1238; Elizabeth Faue, *Community of Suffering and Struggle: Women, Men and the Labor Movement in Minneapolis, 1915–1945* (Chapel Hill: University of North Carolina Press, 1991), 23, 40–45.

3. Federal Writers Project, *Minneapolis: The Story of a City* (St. Paul: Minnesota Department of Education, 1940), 46; Minneapolis Public Schools, *Twenty-Third Annual Report of the Board of Education of the City of Minneapolis*, 1900, 80, 81, 148; Minneapolis Public Schools, *Annual Report*, 1927–1928, 7, 231.

4. *Twenty-Third Annual Report of the Board of Education of the City of Minneapolis*, 71.

5. Minneapolis Public Schools, *Thirty-Third Annual Report of the Board of Education of the City of Minneapolis*, 1910, 63; Minneapolis Public Schools, *Annual Report*, 1924–1925, 40–43; Minnesota Department of Education, *Twentieth Biannual Report of Education*, 1917–1918; C.G. Schulz and W.H. Williams, *Laws Relating to the Public School System Including the State Normal School and the University of Minnesota* (Minneapolis: Syndicate Printing Company, 1915), 56–57; Evelyn Deno and others, *Retarded Youth: Their School Rehabilitation Needs*, Project RD 681, Vocational Rehabilitation Administration, Department of Health, Education, and Welfare, March 1965, 18.

6. Minneapolis Public Schools, *Annual Report of the Board of Education*, 1923–1924, 31, 45.

7. Minneapolis Public Schools, *Annual Report of the Board of Education*, 1924–1925, 13; 1926–1927, 29; 1927–1928, 24.

8. *Annual Report*, 1923–1924, 36, 46.

9. Minneapolis Public Schools, *The Years of Depression, 1930–1935*, 73.

10. Ibid., 13–15, 20; *Annual Report of the Board of Education*, 1927–1928, 7.

11. *Years of Depression*, 156–57.

12. Ibid., 71–88. For the best treatment of how Depression era enrollment increases promoted more functionally oriented curriculum reform, see Jeffrey E. Mirel and David Angus, "The Rising Tide of Custodialism: Enrollment Increases and Curriculum Reform in Detroit, 1925–1940," *Issues in Education* 4 (Fall 1986), 101–20.

13. A.I. Heggerston, "Survey of Special Education in Minneapolis, 1933," 1–2, Minneapolis Board of Education Publications, Minnesota State Archives, Minnesota Historical Society (hereafter SSE).

14. Ibid., 2–3, SSE.

15. Ibid., 45–47, SSE.

16. Ibid., 43–68, SSE.

17. Cutright to Hardaker, March 18, 1932, Special Education, Slow Learning Pupils, 1929–1964 Folder, Minneapolis Public Schools, Information Service Center (hereafter SLP).

18. Wright to Cooley, May 5, 1933, SLP.

19. Greer to McWhorter, May 12, 1933, SLP.

20. Newell to Elementary School Principals, May 25, 1935, SLP; Minneapolis Public Schools, *Curriculum Bulletin No. 171*, September 1935, SLP.

21. Minneapolis Public Schools, "Report on Practices in IB Grade with Slow Learning Pupils as Reported by Seventy IB Teachers," 1936, SLP.

22. Minneapolis Public Schools, *Curriculum Bulletin No. 524*, April 27, 1938, SLP.

23. Minneapolis Public Schools, *Curriculum Bulletin No. 552*, May 26, 1938, SLP.

24. An Experiment with a Small Class of Backward Children, Some of Whom were Anti-Social in Attitudes," June 11, 1937, SLP.

25. Minneapolis Public Schools, "Report of the Small Class or B Curriculum Experiment," January 28, 1949, Minneapolis Board of Education Records, Special Education, Slow Learning Pupils, B Curriculum Folder, Minnesota State Archives, Minnesota Historical Society (hereafter MBER); *Minneapolis Morning Tribune*, January 23,1946.

26. Diane Crew, "English," June 12, 1945, MBER; *Minneapolis Times*, July 28, 1942; June 19, 1946.

27. Hegel to Goslin, May 14, 1945, MBER.

28. Eva Bergeland, "Report of the B Curriculum Department," June 15, 1945, 1–4, MBER.

29. Ibid., 5–6, MBER.

30. Ibid., 5, MBER.

31. Ibid., 4, MBER.

32. "Report of the Small Class, 1, MBER; Folwell Junior High School, "B Curriculum (A Modified Program)," June 3, 1946, MBER.

33. Beauchamp to Gilchrist, January 11, 1947, MBER.

34. Leipold, Everson, and Tallakson to Gilchrist, November 5, 1946, MBER.

35. Minneapolis Public Schools, "Recommendations of the Subcommittee on Learning Materials," March 18, 1947, MBER.

36. Minneapolis Public Schools, "Report of the Policies Subcommittee of the B Curriculum Steering Committee," March 14, 1947, MBER.

37. Minneapolis Public Schools, "Report of the Subcommittee on Implications for the Curriculum in General," March 18, 1947, MBER.

38. Gilchrist to Junior High School Principals, May 12, 1947, MBER.

39. "Report of the Small Class," 3–4, MBER.

40. Minneapolis Public Schools, "Evaluation Committee," July 11, 1947, MBER; Minneapolis Public Schools, "Proposed Evaluation of Small Class Plans," September 22, 1947, MBER.

41. "Report of the Small Class," 7, MBER.

42. Beauchamp to Goslin, June 24, 1948, 2, MBER.

43. Nokomis Junior High School, *Bulletin No. 13*, January 15, 1948, MBER.

44. Franklin Junior High School, "Report on 'Small Classes' Groups," December 6, 1947, MBER.

45. Beauchamp to Gilchrist, June 24, 1948, MBER.

46. *Minneapolis School Bulletin*, June 7, 1951, 3–6.

47. Minneapolis Public Schools, "Minutes of Principals' and Consultants' Workshops," June 25, 1954, SLP; see also Minneapolis Public Schools, "Report of a Sub-Group on Pupil Development and Guidance," July 8, 1947, SLP.

48. Commerce Department, *Seventeenth Census 1950*, vol. 7, part 23 (Washington, D.C.: GPO, 1952), 29, 64; Commerce Department, *Eighteenth Census 1960*, vol. 1, part 25 (Washington, D.C.: GPO, 1963), 60, 68.

49. David J. Leu and John J. McNicholas, Jr., *Planning for the Future: Minneapolis Public Schools* (East Lansing: Michigan State University, 1963) 1:17, 108–12.

50. Minneapolis Public Schools, "Senior High School Principals Meeting," August 28, 1962, SLP.

51. Minneapolis Public Schools, "The Special Problem of the Slow Learner," *Report of Committee IV of the Junior High School Educational Program*, November 20, 1961, SLP; Minneapolis Public Schools, "Some Statements Concerning the Educational Program of the Slow Learner, the Culturally Disadvantaged Pupil and the Potential School Dropout," December 3, 1962, SLP.

52. Minneapolis Public Schools, "Meeting of the Secondary Planning Committee," February 14, 1963, SLP.

53. Friedman to Anderson, June 1, 1964, SLP.

54. Minnesota. *Session Laws of the State of Minnesota Enacted by the State Legislature at the Session Commencing January 8, 1957 and at the Extra Session Commmencing April 20, 1957*, chapter 867–HF No. 121 (St. Paul: Division of Printing, 1957), 1241.

55. Elliot to Superintendents and Directors of Special Education, August 1969, Special Education, Special Classes, Special Learning Disabilities Folder, Minneapolis Public Schools, Information Service Center.

56. Don L. Albertson, "Sister Kenny's Legacy," *Hennepin County History*, 37 (Spring 1978), 3–14; *Minneapolis Board of Education Minutes*, August 28, 1962, Minneapolis Public Schools Information Service Center (hereafter MBM).

57. Minneapolis Public Schools, "Comprehensive Diagnosis and Management of School Children with Subtle Neurological and Sensory Impairments," March 1963, 2–7, Elizabeth Kenny Institute Folder, Minneapolis Public Schools, Information Service Center (hereafter EKI).

58. Deno to Putnam, March 21, 1963, EKI.

59. "Comprehensive Diagnosis and Management," 7, EKI.

60. Ayers to Ellwood and Deno, January 27, 1963, EKI.

61. Harriet Burns, interview, by author, December 12, 1989, Minneapolis.

62. Deno to Tillman, February 1, 1965, EKI.

63. *Minneapolis Tribune*, October 9, 1964.

64. Ibid.

65. *Minneapolis Public School Directory*, 1962–1963, 1963–1964, 1964–1965, 1966–1967, 1970–1971.

66. Carlson to Tillman, May 16, 1967, Reading-Remedial Reading-Miscellaneous, 1966 Folder, Minneapolis Public Schools, Information Service Center.

67. Minneapolis Public Schools, "Elementary Principals Meeting," June 20, 1967, Reading-Remedial Reading-Reading Centers, 1965 Folder, Minneapolis Public Schools, Information Service Center (hereafter RC); Reed to Davis, July 6, 1967, RC.

68. *Minneapolis Board of Education Minutes*, February 27, 1968, MBM.

69. *Minneapolis Tribune*, December 28, 1969; Harriet Burns, John Cumming, and Francis Randall, "Special Learning Disabilities Program and Elementary School Students' Academic Skill Development," Special Education, Special Classes, Special Learning Disabilities, 1970–72 Folder, Minneapolis Public Schools, Information Service Center (hereafter SLD).

70. Deno to Peterson, March 16, 1970, SLD.

71. Burns to Davis, March 20, 1970, SLD; Hansen to Robbinsdale Public Schools, October 20, 1971, SLD; Metzer to Davis, December 22, 1971, SLD.

72. Bress to Davis, April 21, 1971, SLD.

73. Slettehaugh to Davis, April 30, 1971, SLD; Trammel to Davis, May 11, 1971, SLD; Burns to Davis, May 12, 1971, SLD.

74. Davis to Trammel, May 11, 1971, SLD.

75. Gross to Trammel, May 18, 1971, SLD; Davis to Bress, May 19, 1971, SLD.

76. Bress to Davis, October 1, 1971, SLD.

77. Johson to Bress, October 19, 1971, SLD.

78. Bress to Danahy, October 17, 1972, SLD; Bress to Members of the Board of Education, October 18, 1972, SLD.

79. Burns to Gross, June 3, 1971, SLD; Slettehaugh to Davis, July 20, 1971, SLD; Gross to Davis, July 28, 1971, SLD.

80. Gross to Davis, July 28, 1971, SLD.

81. Kennedy to Dabrowkis, September 8, 1971, SLD.

82. Duffy to Burns, January 5, 1972, SLD.

83. Newhall to Taylor Law Firm, Janaury 11, 1972, SLD.

84. Minneapolis Public Schools, "Dr. Davis' Friday Letter to the Board," October 10, 1972, SLD.

85. "General Letter from Planning Committee," December 1971, Groves Learning Center Historical Collection (hereafter GLC); *Minnetonka Sun*, September 28, 1972.

86. *Hartzell Hi-Lights*, September 1977, GLC.

87. *Minnetonka Sun*, September 28, 1972.

88. Ibid.; *Wayzetta Sun*, September 7, 1972.

89. I am indebted to Sue Kirchhoff, Director of the Groves Learning Center, for furnishing me a summary of enrollment statistics and tuition payments from 1972 through 1990.

90. *Minnetonka Sun*, July 8, 1977; April 19, 1978; December 12, 1978.

91. DeVaney to Davis, May 15, 1970, SLD.

92. *Minneapolis Tribune*, June 8, 1969.

93. *Minneapolis Tribune*, June 22, 1969.

Epilogue

1. For a discussion of these social and economic changes and their impact on urban schools, see Harvey Kantor and Barbara Brenzel, "Urban Education and the 'Truly Disadvantaged ': The Historical Roots of the Contemporary Crisis, 1945–1990," *Teachers College Record* 94 (Winter 1992), 278–314; Paul E. Peterson, "The Urban Underclass and the Poverty Paradox," in *The Urban Underclass*, eds. Christopher Jencks and Paul E. Peterson (Washington, D.C.: Brookings Institution, 1991), 3–27; John Rury, "The Changing Social Context of Urban Education: A National Perspective," In *Seeds of Crisis: Public Schooling in Milwaukee Since 1920*, eds. John Rury and Frank Cassell (Madison:University of Wisconsin Press, 1993), 10–41; William Julius Wilson, *The Truly Disadvantaged: The Inner City, the Underclass, and Public Policy* (Chicago: University of Chicago Press, 1987), 20–92.

2. Congress, House of Representatives, Select Committee on Children, Youth, and Families, *U.S. Children and Their Families: Current Conditions and Recent Trends, 1989*, 101st Cong., 1st sess., September 1989 (Washington, D.C.: GPO, 1989), x.

3. Ibid., 54–55, 100–101, 108–9.

4. Joy G. Dryfoos, *Adolescents at Risk: Prevalence and Prevention* (New York: Oxford University Press, 1990), 82–88; David A. Hamburg, *Today's Children: Creating a Future for a Generation in Crisis* (New York: Time Books, 1992), 41–43; Carnegie Council on Adolescent Development, *Turning Points: Preparing American Youth for the 21st Century* (New York: Carnegie Corporation, 1989), 27–32.

5. Dryfoos, *Adolescents*, 236–37; Gary Wehlage, Gregory Smith, and Pauline Lipman, "Restructuring Urban Schools: The New Futures Experience," *American Educational Research Journal* 29 (Spring 1992), 53.

6. For a description of these programs, see Gary Natriello, Ed-

ward L. McDill, and Aaron M. Pallas, *Schooling Disadvantaged Children: Racing against Catastrophe* (New York: Teachers College Press, 1990), 71–137; and Nancy A. Madden and Robert E. Slavin, "Effective Pullout Programs for Students At Risk," in Slavin, Karweit, and Madden, *Effective Programs*, 52–72.

7. Hamburg, *Today's Children*, 240–44; Fred M. Hechinger, *Fateful Choices: Healthy Youth for the 21st Century* (New York: Hill and Wang, 1992), 53–56.

8. Gary Wehlage and others, *Reducing the Risk: Schools as Communities of Support* (London: Falmer Press, 1989), 75–112.

9. Hechinger, *Fateful Choices*, 56–68; Joy Dryfoos, "Schools as Places for Health, Mental Health, and Social Services," *Teachers College Record* 94 (Spring, 1993), 540–67.

10. Wehlage, Smith, and Lipman, "Restructuring," 60–61.

11. H. Craig Heller, "At the Crossroads: Voices from the Carnegie Conference on Adolescent Health," *Teachers College Record* 94 (Spring 1993), 645–52.

12. Hopfenberg and others, *Middle Schools* 43–47; Henry M. Levin, "Financing the Education of At-Risk Students," *Educational Evaluation and Policy Analysis* 11 (Spring 1989), 54; *Accelerated Schools* 1 (Winter 1991), 1, 10–11, 14–15.

13. Jeannie Oakes, Adam Gamoran, and Reba N. Page, "Curriculum Differentiation: Opportunities, Outcomes, and Meanings," in *Handbook of Research on Curriculum*, ed. Philip W. Jackson (New York: Macmillan, 1992), 570–608. See also Jeannie Oakes, *Keeping Track: How Schools Structure Inequality* (New Haven: Yale University Press, 1985); and James Rosenbaum, *Making Inequality: The Hidden Curriculum of High School Tracking* (New York: John Wiley, 1976).

14. Gail P. Kelly, "Setting the Boundaries of Debate about Education," in *Excellence in Education: Perspective on Policy and Practice*, eds. Philip G. Altbach, Gail P. Kelly, and Lois Weis (Buffalo: Prometheus Books, 1985), 35–37.

15. William Bennett, *The De-Valuing of America: the Fight for Our Culture and Our Children* (New York: Summit Books, 1992), 61–62; Chester E. Finn, Jr., *We Must Take Charge: Our Schools and Our Future* (New York: Free Press, 1991), 218–19; Diane Ravitch,

The Schools We Deserve: Reflections on the Educational Crisis of Our Time (New York: Basic Books, 1985), 58–74, 277–78; Diane Ravitch and Chester E. Finn, Jr., *What Do Our 17-Year Olds Know?* (New York: Harper and Row, 1988), 168–72.

16. Alan Gartner and Dorothy Kerzner Lipsky, "Beyond Special Education: Toward a Quality System for All Students," *Harvard Educational Review* 57 (November 1987), 368–69; H. Rutherford Turnbull and Ann Turnbull, *Free Appropriate Public Education: Law and Implementation* (Denver: Love Publishing, 1978), 12–16, 255–63.

17. Alan Abeson, *A Continuing Summary of Pending and Completed Litigation Regarding the Education of Handicapped Children*, no. 6 (Arlington: Council for Exceptional Children, 1973).

18. *The Education for All Handicapped Children Act (P.L. 94–142)*, 20 U.S.C., Sec. 1412; *Federal Register* 42 (August 23, 1977), sec. 121a.550–121a.551.

19. The way that state education managers reported their placement data to the federal government before 1984 made it difficult to assess the actual extent of integration. Children were counted as being placed in one of four settings: regular classes, separate classes, separate schools, and other environments. Using such categories, children who spent some time of the day outside the regular classroom in so-called resource room programs were often counted by states as being placed in regular classrooms. Beginning in 1984, Congress mandated a more detailed reporting of placements by increasing the number of environments to include, among others, resource rooms. With the resource room included, it appears that only twenty-six percent of all handicapped children and sixteen percent of learning disabled children were being served in regular classrooms. Over sixty percent of all handicapped children and eighty percent of learning disabled children were removed from regular classrooms at least part and perhaps all of the day. See Department of Education, *Third Annual Report to Congress on the Implementation of Public Law 94–142: The Education for All Handicapped Children Act* (Washington, D.C.: U.S. Department of Education, 1981), 54; Department of Education, *Seventh Annual Report to Congress on the Implementation of Public Law 94–142: The Education for All Handicapped Children Act* (Washington, D.C.: U.S. Department of Education, 1985), 232–33; Department of Education, *Ninth Annual Report to Congress on the Implementation of the Education of the Handicapped Act* (Washington, D.C.: U.S. Department of Education, 1987), 17–21.

20. Congress, House of Representatives, Subcommittee on Education, *Hearings Before the Select Subcommittee on Education of the Committee on Education and Labor on H.R. 70*, 93rd Cong., 2nd sess., March 6, 7, 8, 22, 1974 (Washington, D.C.: GPO, 1974), 364.

21. The literature on the Regular Education Initiative (REI) is extensive. I have drawn my account from the following: Dorothy Kerzner Lipsky and Alan Gartner, "The Current Situation," in *Beyond Separate Education: Quality Education for All*, eds. Dorothy Kerzner Lipsky and Alan Gartner (Baltimore: Paul H. Brookes Publishing, 1987), 255–89; M. Stephen Lilly, "The Regular Education Initiative: A Force for Change in General and Special Education," *Education and Training in Mental Retardation* 23 (December 1988), 250–60; Maynard Reynolds and Margaret C. Wang, "Restructuring 'Special' School Programs: A Position Paper," *Policy Studies Review* 2 (January 1983), 189–212; Susan Stainback and William Stainback, "The Merger of Special and Regular Education: Can It Be Done? A Response to Lieberman and Mesinger," *Exceptional Children* 51 (April 1985), 517–21; Madeleine C. Will, "Educating Children with Learning Problems: A Shared Responsibility," *Exceptional Children* 52 (February 1986), 411–15. For a review and evaluation of REI, see Thomas M. Skritic, *Behind Special Education: A Critical Analysis of Professional Culture and School Organization* (Denver: Love Publishing, 1991), 51–84.

22. James M. Kauffman, "The Regular Education Initiative as Reagan-Bush Education Policy: A Trickle-Down Theory of Education of the Hard-to-Teach," *Journal of Special Education* 23 (Fall 1989), 256–78. For another critique of REI, see Glenn A. Vergason and M.L. Anderegg, "Preserving the Least Restrictive Environment," in *Issues in Special Education*, eds. William Stainback and Susan Stainback (Boston: Allyn and Bacon, 1992), 45–53.

23. Judith D. Singer and John A. Butler, "The Education for All Handicapped Children Act: Schools as Agents of Social Reform," *Harvard Educational Review* 57 (May 1987), 130.

24. For a good example of the difficulties that contemporary researchers encounter in making a compelling case for the neurological origins of learning disabilities, see Carl W. Cotman and Gary S. Lynch, "The Neurobiology of Learning and Memory," in *Learning Disabilities: Proceedings of the National Conference*, eds. James F. Kavanagh and Tom J. Truss, Jr. (Parkton: York Press, 1988), 1–69.

25. Carrier, *Learning Disability*, 23–54; Coles, *Learning Mystique*, 79–90; Barry M. Franklin, "From Brain Injury to Learning Disability: Alfred Strauss, Heinz Werner, and the Historical Development of the Learning Disabilities Field," in *Learning Disability: Dissenting Essays*, ed. Barry M. Franklin (London: Falmer, 1987), 29–42.

26. Barry M. Franklin, "Introduction: Learning Disability and the Need for Dissenting Essays," in *Learning Disability*, 1–3; Kenneth A. Kavale, "On Regaining Integrity in the LD Field," *Learning Disabilities Research* 2 (Summer 1987), 60–61. For the difficulties facing educators in trying to identify the nature of this condition, see Barbara K. Keogh, "Learning Disabilities: In Defense of a Construct," *Learning Disabilities Research* 3 (Winter 1987), 4–9, and Heinz-Joachim Klatt, "Learning Disabilities: A Questionable Construct," *Educational Theory* 41 (Winter 1991), 47–60.

27. Rebecca Daily Kneedler and Daniel Hallahan, eds., "Research in Learning Disabilities: Summaries of the Institutes," *Exceptional Education Quarterly* 4 (Spring 1983), 1–114.

28. Barbara Keogh, "A Lesson from Gestalt Psychology," Ibid., 122.

29. James D. McKinney, "Contributions of the Institutes for Research on Learning Disabilities," Ibid., 139.

30. Ibid., 136–39.

31. Ibid., 145.

32. Frederick J. Weintraub and Bruce A. Ramirez, *Progress in the Education of the Handicapped and Analysis of P.L 98–199: The Education of the Handicapped Act Amendments of 1983* (Reston: Council for Exceptional Children, 1985), 8.

33. Increasingly, policy scholars are arguing that the best strategy for assisting at-risk groups is an indirect one that provides social supports for all individuals, not just those in need. There is, in fact, a growing movement that is calling for the replacement of targeted welfare policies that are directed solely at the poor in favor of universalistic policies that provide a social safety need for the entire citizenry. See Wilson, *Truly Disadvantaged*, 109–24; and Theda Skocpol, "Targeting within Universalism: Politically Viable Policies to Combat Poverty in the United States," in *The Urban Underclass*, 411–36. For a defense of universalistic social welfare policies on de-

mocratic grounds, see Mickey Kaus, *The End of Equality* (New York: Basic Books, 1992).

34. Natriello, McDill, and Pallas, *Schooling*, 157.

35. Ibid., 158–63.

36. Wehlage, Smith, and Lipman, "Restructuring," 66–69.

37. For a discussion of the moral imperative underlying the ideal of common schooling, see William J. Reese, "Public Schools and the Common Good," *Educational Theory* 38 (Fall 1988), 431–40.

Bibliographical Note

This brief bibliographical note does not mention all the sources that I used in writing this book. The chapter footnotes provide a complete citation of all of my references. My intent here is to highlight those primary and secondary sources that I found most useful in writing this book and which I would recommend to others who are conducting research on the history of educational programs for children with learning difficulties.

There is, unfortunately, no one key collection of primary sources on the education of low-achieving children. Rather, those sources are scattered in a number of places. In writing this book, I relied primarily on a number of public school archives, the papers of philanthropic organizations involved in school reform and child welfare, newspapers, the proceedings of educational associations, and an array of government records. My interpretation of the development of early twentieth-century special education was based on my reading of historical records of the Atlanta Public Schools, some of which are housed in the system's Archives and some of which are located at the Board of Education. I also used the records of the Detroit Board of Education, which are housed in the Board's headquarters, and the records of the New York Public Schools, which are housed in the Special Collections Department of Milbank Memorial Library at Teachers College, Columbia University. In addition to the New York Public School records,

Milbank houses an extensive collection of public school courses of study that offers the researcher a view of the numerous accommodations that public schools undertook for children with learning difficulties. I found courses of study for special and remedial education from Atlanta, Detroit, Minneapolis, and San Francisco to be particularly useful for my work. Of particular help in constructing the early history of special education was the *Proceedings of the National Conference on the Education of Backward, Truant, and Delinquent Children.* A forerunner of the National Council of Social Work, the Conference's annual proceedings describe in great detail the effort of early twentieth-century educators to devise programs for low-achieving, intellectually normal children.

For my description of the array of public school remedial programs in the years after 1930, including the appearance of accommodations for learning disabled children, I turned to the historical records of the Minneapolis Public Schools. Housed both at the Information Service Center of the Board of Education and at the Minnesota State Archives in the Minnesota Historical Society, I found these records to be particularly extensive and useful for understanding the interplay among administrators, teachers, and parents in the education of children with learning difficulties. Also useful in this regard was the Groves Learning Center Historical Collection, which chronicles the development of one of Minneapolis's independent day schools for learning disabled children. For my discussion of the present status of special education, I relied heavily on government documents related to the enactment of Public Law 94–142, the Education for All Handicapped Children Act. Most helpful in this regard were the Senate and House hearings throughout the 1970s on P.L. 94–142 and the annual reports to the Congress from the late 1970s through the 1980s on the implementation of this act.

In describing the efforts of the Atlanta Junior League to promote the education of speech impaired and learning disabled children, I turned to the collections of the Atlanta Speech School and the Atlanta Junior League, which are housed at the Atlanta Historical Society. I also used the Association of Junior Leagues of America Collection located at the Social Welfare

History Archives at the University of Minnesota-Twin Cities. If there is any one archive that a researcher interested in childhood learning difficulties and other disabilities should consult, it is the Social Welfare History Archives. Its extensive collection of organizations and individuals involved in child-saving activities is indispensable for research in this area. It was often difficult to link the development of programs for low-achieving children with the larger process of state-building, which I describe in this volume. Daily newspapers, including the *Atlanta Constitution*, *Atlanta Journal*, and *Minneapolis Tribune* were particularly helpful in this regard. Also useful in making this connection were state government records, in this case the annual reports of the Georgia and Minnesota Departments of Education and the enactments of the Georgia and Minnesota state legislatures.

The most important primary sources in my interpretation of the history of learning disabilities were the array of studies on brain-injured children that Heinz Werner and Alfred Strauss published in various psychological and medical journals during the late 1930s and early 40s. Also useful in understanding the history of learning disabilities is the 1963 *Proceedings of the Conference on Exploration into the Problems of Perceptually Handicapped Children*, the public hearings before the House of Representatives on the 1969 Children with Learning Disabilities Act, and the writings of such founding theorists of the learning disabilities field as William Cruickshank, Samuel Kirk, Newell Kephart, and Samuel Orton.

There are no secondary sources that completely examine the development of school programs for low-achieving children. I did find two studies on the history of the mental hygiene movement helpful in exploring one of the first efforts of early twentieth-century reformers to use the schools for therapeutic purposes. They are Margo Horn's *Before It's Too Late: The Child Guidance Movement in the United States, 1922–1945* (Philadelphia: Temple University Press, 1989) and Theresa Richardson's *The Century of the Child: The Mental Hygiene Movement and Social Policy in the United States and Canada* (Albany: State University of New York Press, 1989). The best sources on the history of special education include Joseph

Tropea, "Bureaucratic Order and Special Children: Urban Schools, 1890s–1940s," *History of Education Quarterly* 27 (Spring 1987), 29–53, and his follow up article, "Bureaucratic Order and Special Children: Urban Schools, 1950s–1960s," *History of Education Quarterly* 27 (Fall 1987), 339–61. Also helpful in this regard was Marvin Lazerson's essay entitled "The Origin of Special Education," which appeared in Jay Chambers and William Hartman's edited volume, *Special Education Policies: Their History, Implementation, and Finance* (Philadelphia: Temple University Press, 1983) and E. Anne Bennison's doctoral dissertation, "Creating Categories of Competence: The Education of Exceptional Children in the Milwaukee Public Schools, 1908–1917" (University of Wisconsin-Madison, 1988).

I found two recent critiques of the learning disabilities field helpful in developing my understanding of the current crisis in learning disabilities research. They are James Carrier, *Learning Disability: Social Class and the Construction of Inequality in American Education* (Westport: Greenwood Press, 1986) and Gerald Coles, *The Learning Mystique: A Critical Look at "Learning Disabilities"* (New York: Pantheon, 1987). For the current state of special education, see Judith D. Singer and John A. Butler, "The Education for All Handicapped Children Act: Schools as Agents of Social Reform," *Harvard Educational Review* 57 (May 1987), 125–52 and Alan Gartner and Dorothy Kerzner Lipsky, "Beyond Special Education: Toward a Quality System for All Students," *Harvard Educational Review* 57 (November 1987), 367–95.

There is today a growing body of literature on the problem of at-risk children. For the best overview of this issue, see Joy Dryfoos, *Adolescents at Risk: Prevalence and Prevention* (New York: Oxford University Press, 1990) and David A. Hamburg, *Today's Children: Creating a Future for a Generation in Crisis* (New York: Time Books, 1992).

I explain the origins of school programs for low-achieving children by looking first at the emergence of a medicalized discourse for talking about childhood deviance and then at the state-building efforts of turn-of-the-century American school reformers. There is an extensive body of secondary literature on both subjects. I found the work of the French philosopher Michel Foucault most helpful in describing the appearance on the scene of this medicalized discourse. See especially his *Discipline and Punish: The Birth of the Prison* (New York: Vintage, 1977) and several of his essays in *Power/Knowledge: Selected Interviews and Other Writings* (New York: Pantheon, 1980) and *Politics, Philosophy, Culture: Interviews and Other Writings, 1977–1984* (New York: Routledge, 1988). Also helpful in constructing this argument was Stanley Cohen and Andrew Scull's edited volume, Social Control and the State (Oxford: Basil Blackwell, 1983), Joan Busfield's *Managing Madness: Changing Ideas and Practices* (London: Unwin Hyman, 1986), and Peter Conrad and Joseph Schneider's *Deviance and Medicalization: From Badness to Sickness*, expanded ed. (Philadelphia: Temple University Press, 1992).

In developing my discussion on state-building, I relied heavily on Peter Evans, Dietrich Rueschemeyer, and Theda Skocpol's edited volume, *Bringing the State Back-In* (Cambridge: Oxford University Press, 1985) and on Thomas Popkewitz's *A Political Sociology of Educational Reform: Power/Knowledge in Teaching, Teacher Education, and Research* (New York: Teachers College Press, 1991). For the history of American state building, see Stephen Skowronek, *Building a New American State: The Expansion of National Administrative Capacities, 1877–1920* (Cambridge: Cambridge University Press, 1982). In linking my discussion of the state to that of private philanthropy, I found two essays to be particularly helpful. One was Lester Salamon's "Of Market Failure, Voluntary Failure, and Third Party Government: Toward a Theory of Government-Nonprofit Relations in the Modern Welfare State," in *Shifting the Debate: Public/Private Sector Relations in the Modern Welfare State*, eds. Susan A. Ostrander and Stuart Langton (New Brunswick: Transaction Books, 1987), 31–37. The other is Beth Stevens's, "Blurring the Boundaries: How the Federal Government has Influenced Welfare Benefits in the Private Sector," in *The Politics of Social Policy in the United States*, eds. Margaret Weir, Ann Shola Orloff, and Theda Skocpol (Princeton: Princeton University Press, 1988), 123–48.

Finally, the argument advanced in this book rests on a belief in common schooling as the best way to accommodate children with learning difficulties. There is an extensive literature on the mid-nineteenth-century common school movement. For the best discussion of the ethical legacy of this movement, see William J. Reese, "Public Schools and the Common Good," *Educational Theory* 38 (Fall 1988), 431–40.

Index

Administration, school: facilitation aspect of, 144; legitimation of profession, 37; progressive, 6, 35; response to low-achieving students, 26, 70; specialized, 37–38; state-building efforts of, 32, 112, 128, 137, 141

Alabama Foundation to Aid Aphasoid Children, 64

Alexia, 62

Alienation, 4

American Association on Mental Deficiency, 50

American Missionary Society, 25

American Psychiatric Association, 52, 56

Amory, Cleveland, 81

Anderson, Wayne, 122, 123

Annie E. Casey Foundation, 143

Aphasia, 59, 68, 92, 94

Aphasoid syndrome, 65

Arnall, Ellis, 98

Association for Children with Learning Disabilities, 65

Atlanta school system, 23–48

Babinski reflex, 50

Beauchamp, Mary, 120

Behavior: adaptive, 47; deficits in, 66; development, 10; disorders, 133; disturbed, 124; modification, 12; self-regulation, 11; social, 112, 151

Behaviorism, 59

Bergeland, Eva, 113, 114, 115, 120

Bodine, William, 14, 15

Brain injury, 15, 18, 48, 51–52, 54, 67, 94, 125, 149; and anoxia, 57; behavioral indicators, 58–59; and cerebral dominance, 62–63, 74; diagnosing, 52, 56, 57, 58, 59, 61; education in, 60, 63; indicators, 60, 61; indirect evidence of, 60; neurological signs, 50, 57, 60; and normal intelligence, 60, 61; parental educational efforts, 63–65; and reading skills, 62

Brittain, M.L., 38, 40

Burns, Harriet, 124–125, 129

Burt, Struthers, 81

Campbell, Isoline, 82

Carlson, Mildred, 126–127

Carrison, Doris, 53

Center for Educational Statistics, 141

Central nervous system: correlates of learning problems, 124; dysfunction, 4, 48, 49, 76; impairment, 125, 126

Cerebral palsy, 60, 92, 100

Children, at-risk: accommodation of, 3; conceptualizing, 149–153; curriculum integration for, 144; defining, 4; interest of educators in, 140